To
Frank
I hope you enjoy
this book
Harry

THEY LED THE WAY

THEY LED THE WAY:

THE CREATORS OF JEWISH AMERICA

Harry A. Ezratty

OMNI ARTS, INC., Publishers
Baltimore, Maryland & San Juan, Puerto Rico

Related Title by the Author

500 Years in the Jewish Caribbean

Other Titles by Author

How to Qualify for Multi-Bar Practice
The Seaman's Handbook of Rights
How to Collect & Protect Works of Art

They Led The Way: The Creators of Jewish America

First Printing: Sept. 1999
ISBN: 0-942929-15-2
Printed In Hong Kong

Omni Arts, Inc.
2 West Read St #150
Baltimore, Md. 21201
1-888-964-BOOK
www.omnititles.com

Cover text excerpted from George Washington's letter to the New Port
(Rhode Island) synagogue:

… while every one shall sit in safety under his own vine and figtree, and there shall be none to make him afraid. May the father of all mercies scatter light and not darkness in our paths, and make us all in our several vocations useful here, and in his own due time and way everlastingly happy.

(signed) G. Washington

*Dedicated to Loren and Eliana,
may they never forget their heritage.*

Acknowledgements

Books are never written in a vacuum. They are the products not only of the author, but of those around him who assist in the process of creating the final work. Because that is so, I offer thanks to the following individuals:

To Dr. Jonathan D. Sarna, Joseph H. and Bella R. Braun Professor of American Jewish History at Brandeis University, my thanks for his insight and suggestions about my manuscript. I thank him also for pointing me in the right direction with respect to understanding events in our history in their proper perspective.

I would not have embarked upon this work without the dedicated prodding of my wife Barbara, who not only urged me to complete this book, but also doubled as its editor.

To my stepsons, Richard and Robert Gottesman, who worked patiently with me on the design of the book's cover;

To Alan Hirsch of Matiz Imaging, who has acted so often as graphics expert for the covers of Barbara's many books and my previous book on Caribbean Jews;

To Laura Peimer, photo archivist of the American Jewish Historical Society, who was instrumental in helping us locate many of the images used to illustrate the book; and

To Iris Blankman, for her patience in proofreading and suggestions that lead to easier reading.

TABLE OF CONTENTS

INTRODUCTION

I'm a New Yorker. Not long ago, while discussing American history with a friend from the South, we talked about the Civil War. I brought up Judah P. Benjamin and his highly visible role with the Confederate States of America.

"They called him 'The Brains of the Confederacy,' " I said. Then I felt foolish. As a Southerner, a Jew and a man in his 60s, my friend probably knew more about Benjamin than I.

"Not only did I not know that," my friend replied, "but I don't even know who the man is."

Like my friend, many American Jews are either unaware of or have only a slight understanding of the role Jews played in America before and during the Civil War. There is a tendency to believe that role begins with the Great Migrations of 1880 to 1920. Most of us can trace our grandparents or great-grandparents to that time in America, so we begin there. But there is a rich history pre-dating that exciting movement from Europe.

We should be aware that early American Jews are as important a part of America's history as are the sons and daughters of later arrivals - the people we all celebrate as American innovators such as Edna Ferber, George Gershwin, Jonas Salk, and Henry Kissinger, to name a few.

Some historians tell us there is no significant Jewish history in early America. True, there were only six Jewish communities in all of North America during the American Revolution: Montreal, New York, Newport, Philadelphia, Charleston and Savannah. But numbers alone don't define quality and importance.

Early American Jews laid the groundwork for those who followed. It was they who set the tone for communal life and religious freedom in this new, raw country. And it was their stories of freedom and opportunity that were whispered about in the cramped ghettos of Europe to people filled with fear and frustration, that lured them across the Atlantic to a new and better life.

The purpose of this book is to reintroduce us to a group of fascinating men and women. Possibly, we will discover some unfamiliar names and begin to appreciate their accomplishments and their significant contributions to the religious and civil freedoms we enjoy today.

There is much to discover and rediscover. How many of us know that it was a Jewish naval officer who abolished flogging in the United States Navy? Or that an American attempted to establish a Jewish homeland in this country 50 years before Theodore Herzl predicted there would someday be one in Palestine? Or that the idea of public charity got its start from the will of a Jewish philanthropist?

This book covers America from Colonial times to the Civil War. Although the Civil War is not generally considered early-American history, the men and women written about did much of their important work earlier, even if their contributions included events during the War.

There is one non-Jew profiled in this book. He belongs here because of his important contribution to religious freedom, not just for Jews but for all Americans. Thomas Kennedy worked to remove the civil disabilities of Maryland's Jews even though when he began his crusade, he knew not one.

It is my hope that readers will not only care about the men and women featured in this book, but they will want to learn more about the others who appear within its pages as well. This is not a scholar's book, but one that points out forgotten events in American Jewish history. Knowing how important religious and civil freedoms and rights were to our ancestors helps us to better appreciate them - and what they did for us - today.

Harry A. Ezratty
Baltimore, Maryland
1999

AMERICA BEFORE THE CIVIL WAR

In 1860, the year before the Civil War, only 150,000 Jews lived in all the United States and its territories. One hundred thousand of them were newcomers, having arrived little more than a decade earlier. They were refugees from revolutions that were tearing Germany and the Austro-Hungarian Empire apart. Of the remaining 50,000, many were descendants of the families who had lived in North America for several generations. The rest were immigrants of the 1840-1850 period.

Before 1840, America's population remained serenely static and insular. There was little immigration of any sort, Jewish or Christian. The decades after the Revolutionary War yielded less than 500 Jewish immigrants yearly. As late as 1840, only 15,000 lived in the United States. For the most part, they gathered in urban communities strung out along the Atlantic coast from New England to Savannah, Georgia. Many Jews had close family or commercial ties with each other. The entire population of the United States just before the Civil War numbered about 25 million. America's Jews counted for much less than one-half of one percent of the total population.

From New England to Georgia, from bustling port cities to the great Mississippi River and across to the settlements of the growing West, no Jewish institution or organization spoke in one voice for America's Jews. There were no Defense Leagues or organized communal charities. Nor were there individual

Jewish spokesman. Unlike older Europe, young America's Jews had few charismatic personalities who spoke for them. There were no leaders politicians could approach to get a sense of Jewish thought.

Before the Civil War, religious leaders Isaac Leeser and Isaac Mayer Wise came closest to being national spokesmen. But both were busy organizing communities and encouraging the establishment of new synagogues. Leeser was dedicated to stemming the rush of the Reform movement, among other things. He did not believe Jews should act in groups for political gains, but only as individuals. Wise, on the other hand, spent much of his time fostering Reform. Neither of these men, despite their importance and stature, spoke for most Jews. Communities had to look within themselves for leaders, for persons who were unique. Often these special people spoke on no-one's behalf.

America also lacked charities, public libraries and the other communal organizations we all now accept as part of American life. Most Americans, Jews and Christians, were newcomers from the same regions of Europe. All were part of the great tide of German immigration to North America before the Civil War.

Many Jewish immigrants cast off European bonds forged of civil disabilities, prejudice and intolerance. They moved quickly into new lives, sometimes passionately. The German Jew, August Bondi, rode with the fiery abolitionist John Brown, hoping to rid America of the shame of slavery. Another German, Simon Baruch, father of financier Bernard Baruch, served with Confederate forces as a combat physician. His fifth generation mother-in-law was a member of the Daughters of the American Revolution.

Of all the immigrants of this period, few equal the political power of Judah P. Benjamin. His career carried him from renowned lawyer to U.S. Senator, then Secretary of War, Justice and State in Jefferson Davis' cabinet of the Confederate States of America. Benjamin was born in the Virgin Islands in 1811.

His family migrated to North Carolina in 1813, then to Charleston a decade later.

American Jews were also undergoing dramatic changes in the practice of their ancient religion. Freed from the strictures of state control over their religious beliefs, they adapted Judaism to America, introducing English into services. The Reform movement was growing. The idea of the religious school took on a new meaning. Orthodoxy was rejected or at least modified, giving rise to conflicts that continue to this day.

During the 1840s and 1850s, America was torn between slavery and its abolition. Politicians tried compromise; both sides fought real battles. Nationally known leaders such as Henry Ward Beecher and Lloyd Garrison attacked slavery in newspapers and the pulpit.

Similar conflicts roiled within Jewish communities. Southern rabbis accepted slavery. With notable exceptions, Northern rabbis considered it a stain on America. No Rabbinical Council or other organization represented regional positions on slavery or secession. Rabbis spoke for themselves, often at odds with their congregants.

New York rabbi Morris Jacob Raphall defended slavery, to the outrage of his congregants. In the border state of Maryland, the conflict turned ugly. Baltimore's rifts threatened violence. An outspoken and single-minded abolitionist, Reform rabbi David Einhorn was forced to move to Philadelphia to escape physical harm directed at him and his family. Rabbi Bernard Illowy, his secessionist opponent, also left Baltimore. Illowy sought a pulpit in New Orleans, where he expected to find congregants sympathetic to his views on slavery. These two rabbis were bitter antagonists in the years before the Civil War.

In the early 19th century, the focus of Jewish vigor and culture was centered in America's South. Charleston enjoyed the reputation of refinement and religious tolerance. Reform scored its first success in the Western Hemisphere in this city. In Charleston, Isaac Harby ran a renowned progressive school, one of America's finest. In Warrentown, North Carolina, Jacob Mordecai ran the country's finest woman's academy. The South enjoyed good theatre, opera and the arts. Its children, Jewish or otherwise, enjoyed the best classical education available in America.

Before the War, Southern Jews were easily accepted within their society, more so than their northern cousins were in theirs. Historian Bertram W. Korn points out that Jews in early New Orleans faced little or no discrimination. They were founders and members of the city's most elite clubs and societies. But in the century after the Civil War, the South had a reputation for being inhospitable to Jews. The misfortunes that were to later befall Southern Jews resulted from the xenophobia of a defeated South. Jews were not the only ones to suffer. Blacks, Yankee carpetbaggers and other "foreigners" felt the same sting. In the Antebellum South, Jews were often called "Israelites" or "Hebrews." These were polite terms generally used with respect. After the War, the word "Jew" supplanted the others and was considered offensive, and Korn reminds us that the same clubs founded by Jews in New Orleans 160 years ago now exclude them.

Raphael J. Moses, who served with the Confederacy in the Civil War as a Major, enjoyed a successful pre-War career as a politician and lawyer. He sat in the Georgia legislature and was for a time, Speaker of the House. He practiced law in Georgia and Florida. In his memoirs, Moses explains changing differences in Southern attitudes towards Jews. A descendant of Colonial settlers, he was a dedicated Southerner. A letter written by him in 1878 would become famous in American History. It would probably never have been written before the War. Moses answered a political opponent who vilified him for being a Jew. Stumping for a colleague who was running for Congress when he received the insult, Moses wrote and published his letter, which proclaimed pride in his faith.

Time was running out for Moses and other Southern Jews.

Before the War, he represented the non-Jews of his district. After the War, he could not get an appointment as judge to the City Court at a salary of $1,200 annually. Several years later, he ran unsuccessfully as County Treasurer. In his memoirs, Moses tells us:

"A young man by the name of Cook belonged to various societies opposed me successfully. I made no personal canvas, asked no man to vote for me and staid (sic) at home on the day of the election. I rested my claims entirely on my record, and was beaten. An instance of how soon past services are forgotten when the power to grant present favors has departed."

When Moses wrote that his opponent "belonged to various societies," was he hinting that he was a member of the Ku Klux Klan? To understand how swiftly animosity to Jews developed after the War, Moses wrote his famous letter 13 years after Appomatox. He retired from politics a year earlier. He does not explain why, except to allude to 1865, the War's end, as a watershed for him in his political life.

Before the War, Southern Jews were fewer numerically than Northern Jews. Yet proportionally, Southern Jews rose much higher in the ranks of their society and government. They held many important positions. Most newcomers to America, including Jews, settled in northern industrial cities where they scrambled for jobs in factories. It was here, too, that poverty festered. Northerners objected to immigrants who competed for jobs, spoke strange languages, practiced odd customs and were crowded into crumbling, decaying neighborhoods.

The South, by contrast, was agrarian and did not experience similar urban upheaval. Southern Jews traced their families back to Colonial times. They shared both the good and bad times with Christian neighbors, fighting side by side against Indians and the British in two wars. They even shared the same rural occupations. Southern Jews put in with the ruling white class and were accepted for their allegiance and support in matters of States Rights and even slavery.

The first Jews to sit in the American Senate were the Southerners David Levy Yulee of Florida in 1845 and Judah P. Benjamin of Louisiana in 1852. They were picked by their state legislators, as was the practice before the Civil War. They were, in effect, members of the club, representatives of the state's power.

While Benjamin was sitting in the Senate, his cousin Henry Hyams was Lt. Governor of Louisiana. There is no comparison of Jewish political power in the North at this time. It is true that Mordecai Manual Noah did attain important political positions in New York City, but he was an exception.

Major Raphael Moses was entrusted with the gold reserves of the defeated Confederacy; David Camden De Leon, the courageous physician-hero of the battle of Chapultapec during the Mexican American War, was offered the position of the Confederate Army's Surgeon General. North Carolina's Alfred Mordecai, a major in the Union Army and a recognized expert in armaments, was offered the post of Chief Ordnance officer for the Confederacy. These were not men whose talents surfaced a year or two before the War. All had been important to the South for many decades before the Civil War.

Look back to the Revolutionary War and the role of Georgia's Sheftall and Minis families. So involved in the Revolution were Georgia's Jews, that British dispatches specifically mention them as troublesome rebels. It was urged that after the British quelled the rebellion, no more Jews be allowed to live in the Colonies. Some historians believe that David Emmanuel, Georgia's Governor in 1801, was Jewish. If so, it would be more than another century before the next Jew, Moses Alexander of Idaho, would be elected to a statehouse. That was in 1915.

When the shackles of European ghettos were broken, Jewish immigrants were free to come to America and range through the vast spaces of their newly adopted country. Their exploits as backpacking, itinerant peddlers are part of

America's folklore. Trading with Indians, some became part of the tribal family. They stepped into every corner of American life and became readily accepted. Jews were just another immigrant group among dozens. Later, they were asked to assume the task of running pioneer towns as mayors, legislators and even sheriffs and marshals. For they had a great stake in the maintenance of order and stability along the frontier.

One problem facing American Jews at the approach of the 21st century is assimilation. It is not a new concern. Settlers in the rural South or the pioneering communities of Kentucky and Tennessee had been almost certain to give way to the dominant culture, if not in the first generation than most assuredly by the second or third. Only large urban areas could afford rabbis, schools and other religious support groups. In an age lacking electronics and hampered by slow travel across unpaved roads, maintaining religious commitments was difficult.

The reality of American Jewish religious life until 1840 is that it never had an ordained rabbi. Services were led by laymen who stepped in to fill the void. Even the city of Charleston, with America's largest Jewish community, could not find its own rabbi. It offered to pay for the education of any young man who would undertake to become its spiritual leader. There were no takers.

In spite of this, by the time the Civil War approached all of the dedicated people profiled in this book had a part in building the foundations for a positive future for American Jewry.

ASSER LEVY VAN SWILLEM

"...the Jewish Nation here make known, ... how that one of our Nation... requested of the Noble Burgomasters that he might obtain his Burgher's certificate... which to our great surprise was declined and refused ..."

Abraham de Lucena,
leader of the New Amsterdam
Jewish community, 1655

During the waning days of the summer of 1654, the French frigate *St. Charles* sailed up New York harbor. Her destination was the Dutch colony of New Amsterdam at the tip of the island of Manhattan.

Among other cargo, the ship carried twenty-three Jews fleeing from Recife, Brazil, a former Dutch colony recently retaken by the Portuguese, who ordered all Jews out of the colony.

(Although twenty-three has long been used in reference to the number of America's first Jewish immigrants, historians recently have maintained that the number might have been different, perhaps twenty-seven.)

All of the refugees on the *St. Charles* but one were sought by Portugal's Inquisitors. Had they remained in Brazil, they would have been in mortal danger.

Later generations called the *St. Charles* "American Jewry's Mayflower." Unlike the Puritans, however, this small band of refugees did not sail to the New World with royal land grants, patents and official government approval. They were met in New Amsterdam as were all Jews in the 17th century: grudgingly and with suspicion and fear.

History does not tell us if these unfortunate passengers were willing settlers to this Dutch colony of less than 1,000 souls. They were rescued on the high seas from Spanish brigands who had captured them, and taken their property and their children for transport to Havana, never to be recovered. The adults were rescued by French Captain De La Motthe, who insisted the destitute Jews pay the price of passage to New Amsterdam. De La Motthe filed an action at law in the Colonial court when he touched port.

Lacking money to pay the debt, these founders of America's first Jewish community were forced to remain in New Amsterdam until their passage was paid to the court. Letters were sent to family and friends in The Netherlands requesting funds.

One among them was not Sephardic, nor Spanish, nor Portuguese. He was Asser Levy Van Swillem, a Jew from Poland who had migrated to Holland, then to the Dutch colony at Recife. There, he lived and probably traded among the Indians in the Brazilian jungle. Levy was responsible for many Jewish firsts in North America: he was a bold man who asserted his rights. He was the first in America to belong to a militia and stand defense of a community. Levy was also the first to represent the interests of another before an American court. He could be said to be America's first Jewish lawyer. As we shall see, the list goes on. He rose from the most difficult conditions in this colony to become a respected and substantial Burgher in the city of New Amsterdam, later New York.

New Amsterdam's crusty governor, Peter Stuyvesant, wanted no Jews in his city. So he wrote to his Board of Directors in Holland:

"It would not be in the best interests of the general community of your worships that the deceitful race - such hateful enemies and blasphemers of the name of Christ - not be allowed further to infect and trouble this new colony, to the detraction of your worships' most affectionate subjects."

New Amsterdam was less than a decade old. The cantankerous old Stuyvesant was careful to keep Jews from settling in his colony. As careful as he was, he overlooked one who had preceded the unfortunate twenty-three. Jacob Barsimson had landed a few weeks earlier, perhaps with the task of scouting possibilities for settling "Hebrews" there. He was to become closely associated with Levy in the struggle for civil equality. Why Barsimson did not raise Stuyvesant's anger or interest remains an unanswered question. If his mission was to open the door for Jewish immigration, there is no record of the Governor's objection.

Although officially unwelcome, the newcomers did receive sympathy from some of the Dutch settlers, who recognized they had suffered as prisoners of the Spanish pirates, lost their children and were destitute. Indeed the Jews would endure more distress in the harshness of the coming winter. It was these sympathetic colonists who would provide the new settlers with the necessities to carry them past the icy winter until money came from Amsterdam to settle their debts with De La Motthe.

Governor Peter Stuyvesant and his councilors were not so understanding. They did all they could to rid themselves of those they considered the new undesirables. But the Jews fought Stuyvesant, countering his letter with one of their own. They told the Amsterdam directors:

"We have nowhere to go. We cannot return to Spain or Portugal. The Inquisition will kill us; we are all refugees from the Dutch colony of Recife, which each of us defended against the Portuguese with our lives and fortunes; if you will not have us then we will go to the British and French colonies."

Finally, there was a direct appeal to the Board and stockholders of the Dutch West India Company. Amsterdam was home to a number of affluent Jews. Many were associated with the Dutch West India Company as Directors, stockholders and international traders. This last argument probably touched the Dutch pocketbook.

Permission to remain in the colony was granted, based upon loyal service rendered in Recife and that a good number of investors in the company were Jewish. They could live and trade in the colony, the reply said, but it also warned that Jewish poor were to burden neither the colony nor the Company.

Communications were slow in the 17th century. Before the reply was received, Stuyvesant continued making life uncomfortable for his unwanted settlers. His Sheriff arrested one member of the community for keeping a shop open on Sunday. The charge was serious, since it also alleged the offense occurred during a sermon. The Sheriff demanded the offender be fined, reminding the court the Governor wanted all Jews out of his colony. Stuyvesant received the matter for disposition. He took no action, however, since by then he had received instructions from Amsterdam not to trouble the newcomers.

New Amsterdam, later to become New York City, was a tiny enclave at the tip of Manhattan Island. Its southern end, called the Battery, poked into the waters of New York Harbor. Here, the Hudson and East rivers met, washing into the harbor. From here the city grew north to Wall Street, where a wooden stockade was thrown up across the island. The 10-feet high stockade, called the Cingle was built up in response to threats from the New England colonies. The wall also kept out marauding Indians who shared the island with the Dutch.

New Amsterdam was also open to attack along both of its rivers. On the banks of the East River, Stuyvesant built a fortified Water Gate. At Broadway and Wall Streets, a Land Gate guarded the entrance to this little town. To man these defenses, a militia called the Burgher Guard was mustered. It was made up of less than 200 colonists. Their duty was called "Watch and Ward."

Six months after Asser Levy arrived at New Amsterdam, Governor Stuyvesant mounted an expedition to Delaware to recapture a Dutch fort overrun earlier by Swedish settlers. The militia at New Amsterdam now needed more men. Levy and Barsimson petitioned the Colonial Council for the right to bear arms and stand Watch and Ward.

The Council denied the petition, stating *"the disinclination and unwillingness of ...* (the citizens) *to be on guard with them* (Levy and Barsimson) *in the same guardhouse"* as well as their lack of citizenship, prevented their petition from being considered favorably. The Council added, incorrectly, that there was no precedent in the Netherlands for letting Jews stand Watch and Ward.

In addition to denying the request, the Council dealt an unsolicited blow to the petitioners. It decreed that all men between the ages of 16 and 60 unable to bear arms, had to pay a tax instead of rendering service. Levy and Barsimson were ordered to pay the tax. Both men were penniless and unable to comply. They protested, arguing *"We are required to work with our hands, we have no money to pay the tax."* Levy added, *"I defended Recife against the Portuguese."*

The Council was adamant. It answered with contempt:

"Director General and Council persist in the resolution passed, yet as the petitioners are of the opinion that the result of this will be injurious to them, consent is hereby given them to depart whenever and wither it pleases them."

The Council was forced to relent because of pressure from Amsterdam. Shortly thereafter, Levy and Barsimson were admitted to Watch and Ward, becoming the first Jews in the American colonies to exercise the privilege.

Despite their successes, the community still suffered harassment from Stuyvesant and his Council. Although Stuyvesant had clear orders, Abraham de Lucena, Salvador D'Andrada and Jacob Cohen had to remind the capricious governor they already were granted certain rights. The West India Company allowed them to trade as far north as Albany, then called Fort Orange, and south to the Delaware River. Stuyvesant stubbornly denied the petition, but he also hedged. Since they had already begun trading in these regions, the Governor allowed them to send agents to carry on such trade as had already begun. Once again, the Dutch West India Company ordered Stuyvesant to permit Jewish settlers to engage in trade. They were, however, not to conduct their religious service or open retail shops. Nor could they practice a craft. Then, in a curious postscript, Holland suggested that the Jews could live wherever they chose, hoping they might build their houses close to each other. Holland was gently urging Jews to construct their own ghetto. The Jews ignored the suggestion.

New York's Jews did live together in a neighborhood, but not because of any law. By 1729, when Shearith Israel built the first synagogue at Mill Street, that street was the center of the Jewish population. It had formerly been called "Jew Street."

****

One of the highest civic honors anyone could have in New Amsterdam was elevation to the status of a Burgher. It was an ancient privilege granted by European municipalities. It had a long and honorable history, its origins going back to the Middle Ages. Burghers were exempt from certain legal processes and their property was often safe from judicial attachments.

In New Amsterdam, a Burgher could become a property

owner. He had his pick of government land grants as they became available. Levy filed an application for Burgher rights. It was denied. *"You are a Jew, Mynheer,"* he was told by a spiteful councilor. Levy would not accept the rejection. He had been a Burgher in Amsterdam before he sailed to Brazil. He appealed to Stuyvesant, pointing out that he could not be denied a right he had in Holland. This time, he was supported by de Lucena, d'Acosta, Cohen and Abraham Henriques. They were all leaders of the community who had also filed petitions. On April 20, 1657, Asser Levy Van Swillem and the others received the first Burgher certificates issued by an American colony to members of the Jewish faith.

Levy prospered. He earned a reputation among the Dutch and later with the English, as a fair and honest merchant. Later he received the colony's permission to operate a slaughter-house. It was an important personal right, since the municipality closely regulated it. Levy was not required to take the necessary oath on a Christian bible; instead, he used a book containing the Torah. Afterwards, Levy was exempt from having to slaughter pigs, something an observant Jew would find offensive. It was a sign of the sensitivity the Colonial government acquired over the years.

Levy was probably the first Jew to own a Public House in the colonies. He traveled north to the upper reaches of the Hudson River, trading and trapping. His reputation spread beyond the island of Manhattan. He was requested by Jacob Lucena to represent him before the law courts in Hartford, Connecticut. Court records reveal that Levy was not only known in Hartford, but was received there with courtesy and respect. He was able to reduce a large fine that had been previously imposed on Lucena.

Levy was the first Jew in the colonies to become a landowner, not just in Manhattan, but in upstate New York. He owned the land in New York on which the synagogue for America's first Jewish congregation was built. He deeded that land to his congregation, Shearith Israel.

Asser Levy was counted among the wealthiest citizens of New York. He was the first in many things, including helping New York's Lutheran community with money for church construction. It was the first time a Jew helped another religious community.

Asser Levy Van Swillem's story could only have happened in New Amsterdam. Other Dutch colonies throughout North America and the Caribbean welcomed Jewish colonists. They granted civil rights and religious freedom as incentives to encourage their settlement. The Dutch had a well-deserved reputation for liberal administration in their outposts. Only in New Amsterdam did Jews labor under the intolerant Peter Stuyvesant and his acquiescent Councilors. It was not strange, then, that New Amsterdam's Jews were attracted to Surinam, Curaçao and St. Eustatius. On those islands, they not only lived in peace, but they could also build their own synagogues and invite rabbis to minister to them.

Levy, Barsimson and a few others, however, remained in New Amsterdam. Stuyvesant and his administration persistently put obstacles before them. Theirs was an act of defiance not often seen in the 17th century, when most Jews of the world had little civil status. By the time the English acquired New Amsterdam, Levy may have been the only Jew on the island of Manhattan.

Levy's fight was significant for several reasons. In this New World in the Western Hemisphere, he took the position that Jews should not be treated differently from other citizens. He chose to fight in the colony that would become New York City, history's greatest Jewish city, in the country that was to become their greatest haven. But Levy's fight would have been worthless if he had just won and stopped there. Instead, he went on to become a respected and important member of the community, proving that given the opportunity other citizens enjoyed, a Jew could succeed.

This was Asser Levy Van Swillem's legacy to those who followed: he forced a spiteful government to bend to reason and justice and treat Jews with an even hand. Things did not change immediately after the English captured New Amsterdam in 1664 and changed its name to New York. It took an enlightened Duke of York 20 years to remove most of the civil disabilities. But it was Levy who did the hard early work, insisting on citizenship, the right to bear arms to defend his community, and to own land. There is an old adage, "the right person at the right time." Asser Levy was that right person at the right time. He was also at the right place.

Asser Levy has not been forgotten. He was made an immortal son of New York in 1955 when, in his honor, the City dedicated Asser Levy Place, a street not far north of where he once lived. The dedication was part of the celebration of the 300th anniversary of the first Jewish settlement in America, founded in Dutch New Amsterdam. Asser Levy Place runs between 23rd and 25th Streets, near East River Drive, on Manhattan's East Side.

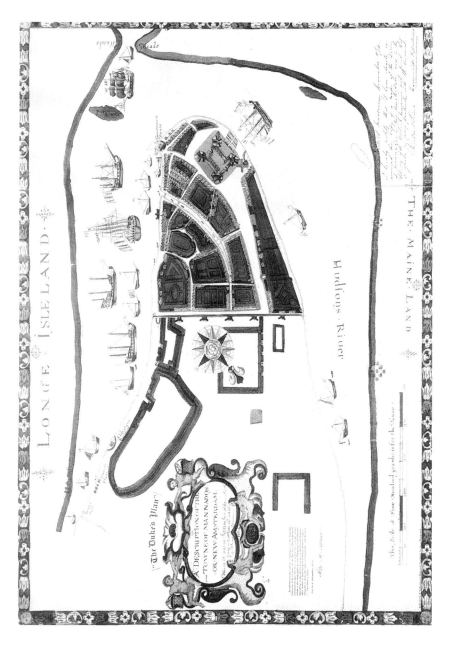

Map of New Amsterdam, c. 1648

Governor Peter Stuyvesant

View of New Amsterdam, 1667

THE JEWISH ARGONAUTS OF NEWPORT

*"I desire not that liberty for myself, which I
would not freely and impartially weight out to
all the consciences of the world beside."*
Roger Williams

In an era when Jews were conceived of as petty merchants, usurers, and generally outside the world of polite commerce, a group of determined Jewish settlers found their way to Colonial New England. They engaged in shipping and whaling, firing up a new American industry born of whale oil and, in so doing, they rose to become some of the wealthiest and most progressive businessmen in America. On the way to their success, they helped dispel some anti-Semitic myths. Almost to a man, they were loyal to the American Revolution and to the democratic ideals it represented. The Jewish Argonauts of Newport tested the waters of American freedom and commerce, becoming examples and ideals for the Jews who followed them.

An Argonaut has been defined as a venturer. The term was applied to the '49ers who drew gold from California's soil. The Newport Argonauts, predating the Californians, ventured into political and economic uncertainty to draw freedom from commerce.

Of all the British colonies in North America, New England's were the most intolerant. Not only were "Israelites" unwelcome, so were Quakers, Catholics and atheists. Lapses of faith by colonists regarding the New Testament's supremacy brought edicts of exile and, sometimes, death.

The freethinking dissenter, Roger Williams, was banished from Massachusetts Bay Colony for his non-conformist religious beliefs. Williams began his career as a minister in the Church of England. Later, he became a Puritan pastor. In 1635, he struggled with his parishioners over whether any punishment should be exacted for certain Sabbath infractions. Williams was ordered exiled *"from the jurisdiction of the Puritans of America, and driven into the wilderness to endure the severity of our northern winter and the bitter pangs of hunger."*

He founded his own colony, Rhode Island and Providence Plantations. His tolerant attitude clearly envisioned a place for Jews in this haven. However, Rhode Island's charter, approved in 1663, limited settlement to those who would *"preserve unto them that liberty in the true Christian faith."*

In 1657, before Rhode Island's incorporation, Moses Pacheco and Mordecai Campanall journeyed northward across the Caribbean from Barbados, to investigate the new colony's potential for settlement. They liked what they saw. Returning to their home in the West Indies, they gathered their families and others who were impressed with their description of the mainland colony. Together, they established the second Jewish colony in North America, and New England's first, in the city of Newport.

Things did not go as expected for the newcomers. Shortly after they arrived, they were tried as aliens by colonial courts. Eventually, they were acquitted of violating England's trading laws.

After Williams' death, the few Jews who continued to live in the colony became subject to harassment by his successors. But the colony's General Assembly obviously considered the presence of Jews to be beneficial: they turned away from the spirit of the law and allowed not only Jewish immigration, but Jewish trade as well. Britain's Parliament stepped in and resolved the dilemma for its American colonies. In 1740, it standardized the process of naturalization for non-British colonials. Any settler with seven years of residence in British America was eligible to apply for naturalization. These new, easy regulations attracted more Jews to the city of Newport. Some were refugees from the Spanish Inquisition, arriving directly from Spain. They strengthened the community. By 1759 there were enough Jews in Newport to plan and fund the building of what is now the Touro Synagogue, the oldest and most revered Jewish house of worship in America. The structure, however, was not America's first synagogue. Shearith Israel's Mill Street Synagogue was erected in 1729 in New York City.

Although Jews lived in Newport for over 100 years before the Revolutionary War, the Jewish Argonauts' greatest impact was in the decades immediately before 1776. The arrival in the mid-18th century of Jacob Rodrigues Rivera and Aaron Lopez, helped make Newport an important center of trade, because they brought with them knowledge of sperm oil manufacture. It grew to become a giant native industry, the first of its type in America. The manufacture of candles and oil, necessary for heat and light at a time when electricity was yet to be harnessed, made Aaron Lopez the greatest merchant in New England. Historian Jacob Rader Marcus tells us that burning one spermaceti candle for five hours daily, for 30 days, cost $16 (based on 1961 value, when Marcus was writing.)

In 1761, James Lucena introduced the manufacture of castile soap to the colony, while other Argonauts engaged in shipping the "Golden Triangle," the trade route that ran from Africa and Europe to the West Indies and North America.

The success of Lopez, Lucena, Rodrigues Rivera and the other Argonauts was the necessary encouragement that brought more Jews to Newport. After a disastrous earthquake in Lisbon in 1756, others came to Newport from Portugal. They also engaged in shipping, rum, molasses, the West Indian trade and slaves. Their numbers were such that Newport may well have been home to Colonial America's largest single Jewish community.

The Newport Jews retained a distinguished architect to design the structure that would one day become famous as the Touro Synagogue. In addition to erecting a building, the congregation realized that they would need the services of a full time Hazzan (cantor). For this position, they hired Isaac Touro. It was Touro's son, Judah, who would later become a renowned philanthropist and endow and ensure the continuation of the synagogue, its congregation and its cemetery.

****

So vital was Aaron Lopez to the economic health of Newport, he became known as "The Merchant Prince of New England." He owned or controlled some 30 ocean going vessels and over 100 coastal ships. With his father-in-law, Jacob Rodriguez Rivera, he introduced and controlled America's sperm oil industry.

Despite his prominence and commercial influence, the Court and Council of Rhode Island refused to apply the British Laws of Naturalization of 1740 when Lopez filed for citizenship. It was a situation somewhat similar to that facing Asser Levy and Jacob Barsimson, 100 years earlier in New Amsterdam. In 1655, Peter Stuyvesant blocked Jews from having civil rights in violation of his own laws. In 1761, Aaron Lopez and Isaac Elizar petitioned the Rhode Island authorities for citizenship and they, too, were denied, in violation of existing laws.

The similarity ends there, however. While Stuyvesant finally relented, and granted Burgher status to New Amersterdam's

Jews, Rhode Island's legal system refused to do so. Aaron Lopez was finally obliged to file for his citizenship in the Province of Massachusetts, thereby becoming the first of his religion to be naturalized in that colony.

Ezra Stiles, president of Yale University, knew Lopez personally. He wrote of him:

"He was a merchant of the first eminence; for honor and extent of commerce probably surpassed by no merchant in America. He did business with the greatest of ease and exactness - always carried about with him a sweetness of behavior, a calm urbanity, and agreeable and unaffected politeness of manners. Without a single enemy and the most universally beloved by an extensive acquaintance of any man I ever knew."

Lopez, Lucena and Rodrigues Rivera were not the only Argonauts. Others like Moses Lopez, Isaac Polock, Jacob Isaacs, Abraham Sarzedas, Naphtali Hart and Moses Levy added to Newport's mercantile prominence. These men organized America's first Jewish men's club. Aside from their interest in business, they belonged to the local Masonic Lodge. There is reason to believe that Masonry was brought to the colonies by the Argonauts. The first accounts of initiation in America go back to 1658 at Mordecai Campanall's home.

The Argonauts were also founders and important supporters of Newport's famous Redwood Library, which functions to this day. They helped support other communal activities in the city and were instrumental in retaining Peter Harrison, Boston's prestigious architect, to build the Touro Synagogue.

Harrison's fame rested with his design and construction of Christ Church in Cambridge and Boston's King's Chapel. His Colonial American structure is a jewel of early American architecture. He designed the synagogue in the Sephardic tradition: congregants face each other on both sides of the synagogue, instead of facing the Holy Ark. The Reader's Table, or Bimah, is positioned between the congregants, facing the Ark several feet away. The Women's Gallery is on the second floor where, according to Orthodox tradition, women sit apart from men.

The mercantile influence of the Jewish Argonauts lasted for barely a quarter century. Much of what they created still remains, however: the Synagogue with its nearby cemetery, the Redwood Library, and the memory and history of Newport as an important trading center and seaport.

This vigorous, productive community was broken up during the Revolutionary War. Almost all the Argonauts supported the Revolution, so British occupation scattered them. Many joined the army, others gave money, their ships and arms to repel the British. When British boots finally trod across Newport's streets, the community fled to safety, some to Leicester, Massachusetts, others to Philadelphia. Newport never regained its importance as an American commercial and trading center. At the War's end, some Argonauts returned to their city. But the commercial position they once enjoyed did not continue. Their pre-eminent head, Aaron Lopez, died in a tragic accident on the road just as he was returning to Newport. Perhaps it was the lack of his dynamic presence, the destruction caused by the British occupation and blockade, or the rise of commerce in New York and Philadelphia that blocked regrowth in Newport. Gradually, the Argonauts drifted away, to enrich other cities with their commercial vigor.

The synagogue virtually ceased operating, although it was eventually to become a revered structure, a national historic site, and to have an illustrious history. A tablet attesting to its role in Rhode Island and American History states:

"Here in 1781-84 the Rhode Island General Assembly met, and during Washington's visit to Newport in 1781 a town meeting was held here. The state supreme court held sessions here at that period."

In 1790, George Washington, president of the United States, visited Newport. Presented with a letter from the congregation written by Moses Seixas, Washington replied in the words that American Jews have since cherished. This letter unequivocally establishes religious freedom as an American principle:

"...The citizens of the United States of America have a right to applaud themselves for having given to mankind examples of an enlarged and liberal policy: a policy worthy of imitation. All profess alike liberty of conscience and immunity of citizenship ... May the Children of the Stock of Abraham who dwell in this land continue to merit and enjoy the good will of the other inhabitants; while everyone shall sit in safety under his own vine and fig tree, and there shall be none to make him afraid. May the father of all mercies scatter light and not darkness in our paths, and make us all in our several vocations useful here, and in his own due time and way everlastingly happy."

* * * * *

The Jewish Argonauts of Newport are not just forgotten names in history books. We remember them through their deeds and their monuments in the old Jewish graveyard of the city. There they lie, with words on the headstones above them carved in English, Hebrew, Spanish and Portuguese. Henry Wadsworth Longfellow forever immortalized them with his 1854 poem, "The Jewish Cemetery at Newport."

In 1852, Longfellow came across the graves while strolling in Newport on a holiday. He was immediately taken with the tranquility of the graveyard and the Hispanic names. A professor of Romance Languages, Longfellow was intrigued by the joining of Hispanic family names with Hebrew first names. This odd coupling led him to seek out the custodian of the cemetery and set him to put his thoughts on paper. On July 9,

1852, he wrote in his diary:

"Went this morning to the Jewish Burying Ground, with Mr. Gould the Tailor, a polite old gentleman who keeps the key. There are but a few graves; nearly all are low tomb-stones of marble; with Hebrew inscriptions and a few words added in English or Portuguese.

"Among the names are Isaac Mendes Seixas; Moses Lopez, Jacob Lopez, Abraham Rodrigues Rivera (in handsome raised letters); Moses Alvarez; and at the foot of each of the letters, S.A.G.D.G. It is a shady nook at the corner of two dusty, frequented streets, with an iron fence, and a granite gateway erected at the expense of Mr. Touro of New Orleans; the tombs of whose ancestors rise rather ostentatiously in the enclosure.

"Over one of the graves grows a weeping willow, from a slip taken from the tree over Napoleon's grave at St. Helena; at two removes - the grand-child of that willow."

So impressed was Longfellow at the stones in this cemetery that early drafts of his poem reveal his understanding of who the Jewish Argonauts were:

"The names upon their monuments are strange,
Of foreign accent and different climes,
Alvarez and Rivera interchange
With Abraham and Jacob of old times.
And with them mingles the forgotten name
That Moses bore engraven on his rod,
The four great letters now no longer heard
The sacred sound, the shuddering name of God."

Longfellow's poem forever reminds us of the Jewish Argonauts. Their fame during colonial times encouraged others to come to America for a better life and try to make their fortunes. The Jewish Argonauts helped to build the city of Newport into an important commercial center. They are not forgotten; their lovely synagogue and cemetery, their enduring community works, and Longfellow's poem have insured their immortality.

Interior, Newport Synagogue, photo © John T. Hopf

Gilbert Stuart portrait of Hazzan Abraham Touro, photo ©
John T. Hopf

To the Hebrew Congregation in Newport—
Rhode Island.

Gentlemen.

While I receive, with much satisfaction, your Address replete with expressions of affection and esteem; I rejoice in the opportunity of assuring you, that I shall always retain a grateful remembrance of the cordial welcome I experienced in my visit to Newport, from all classes of Citizens.

The reflection on the days of difficulty and danger which are past is rendered the more sweet, from a consciousness that they are succeeded by days of uncommon prosperity and security. If we have wisdom to make the best use of the advantages with which we are now favored, we cannot fail, under the just administration of a good government, to become a great and a happy people.

The Citizens of the United States of America have a right to applaud themselves for having given to mankind examples of an enlarged and liberal policy, a policy worthy of imitation. All possess alike liberty of conscience and immunities of citizenship. It is now no more that toleration is spoken of as if it was by the indulgence of one class of people, that another enjoyed the exercise of their inherent natural rights. For happily the Government of the United States, which gives to bigotry no sanction, to persecution no assistance requires only that they who live under its protection should demean themselves as good citizens, in giving it on all occasions their effectual support.

It would be inconsistent with the frankness of my character not to avow that I am pleased with your favorable opinion of my administration, and fervent wishes for my felicity. May the Children of the Stock of Abraham, who dwell in this land, continue to merit and enjoy the good will of the other Inhabitants; while every one shall sit in safety under his own vine and figtree, and there shall be none to make him afraid. May the father of all mercies scatter light and not darkness in our paths, and make us all in our several vocations useful here, and in his own due time and way everlastingly happy.

G Washington

Letter to Newport Congregation from President George
Washington, Photo © John T. Hopf

MORDECAI SHEFTALL

" He is a very great Rebel."
Lt. Col. Archibald Campbell,
Scottish Highlanders

The third oldest Jewish community in colonial America was founded in the steamy seaport city of Savannah, Georgia. In 1731, London's Sephardic community dispatched a boatload of Jews for settlement in that English colony. The London community sought to relieve itself of a glut of European refugees, which it was finding difficult to maintain, because of lack of opportunity for them to find the means to support themselves.

The Christian founders of Georgia colony and its main supporter, James Ogelthorpe, had envisioned a place where all religions except Catholicism would be tolerated. Had no one anticipated Jewish colonists? At first, as in every early American colony, they were unwelcome. The new group of 41 Jewish immigrants persevered, winning the right to set roots in Georgia and become property owners. Although most of the newcomers were of Spanish and Portuguese descent, including some

Italians, at least one of them, Benjamin Sheftall, was Ashkenazic. He acted as interpreter for a group of German settlers who were Lutherans.

Later boatloads of immigrants followed until, as historian Jacob Rader Marcus claims, Georgia had the largest Jewish community in all the colonies in the early 1700s. But economic failures and aggressive raids by Spaniards from across the Florida border reduced the Jewish community to two families, the Minises and the Sheftalls.

Portuguese Jews had much to be concerned about. Many Sephardim had returned to Judaism. Should the Spanish apprehend them, it would mean an appearance before the dreaded Inquisition. It was for this reason that the only two families remaining were Ashkenazim.

Savannah's community was to revive by the 1770s, only to be decimated again by the Revolutionary War. It would renew itself permanently at the War's end. Throughout these difficult times, the Sheftalls became one of the leading families in the South.

Mordecai Sheftall was born in 1735, the first white child to be born in Georgia. He became a soldier during the Revolution, as well as a hero, merchant, and communal and religious leader. He belonged to America as much as any other man who fought for her. Contemporary accounts tell us that Sheftall was probably the most dedicated leader against the English in Georgia. More than half of the colonists in Georgia either vacillated in their support for the Revolution, or were pro-English.

Sheftall was also an important part of Jewish America. His Bar Mitzvah in 1748 was the first such recorded ceremony in North America, according to the Encyclopedia Judaica. He was among the founders of three of America's oldest congregations (Mikveh Israel of Savannah, Mikveh Israel of Philadelphia, and Beth Elohim of Charleston.) Both he and his wife Frances were able to write in Hebrew. When one considers that for the greater part of his life Sheftall lived on the frontier with sometimes only one other Jewish family nearby (and at most, perhaps no more than 15), it is remarkable how this man not only adhered to his religion but was active in fostering it. When Benjamin Sheftall died in 1765, Mordecai assumed the management of the family's holdings. He did well as a merchant, miller and rancher. On the eve of the Revolutionary War he helped reorganize Savannah's Mikveh Israel. He also served as its ritual circumcisor. It was in his home that the Jewish community prayed before they moved into their own house of worship. And it was Sheftall who donated the land dedicated to the community's cemetery. An additional plot of land that he deeded to the congregation, which was located outside the city limits, was sold. Its proceeds would later be used for a community house.

At the outbreak of war, Sheftall had no doubt that he would remain in Georgia to fight against the British. Jacob Rader Marcus, analyzing Sheftall's motives, explains that Sheftall was astute enough to understand that the freedoms America gave Jews were not available elsewhere. In addition, Sheftall was not British. His father was German, and Sheftall grew up as a settler far from an England that he had briefly visited once. America was his home. And it was made up not only of the English, but of Spanish, German and other settlers as well. America was a place where most residents came from somewhere other than England and where people were too busy to concern themselves with a man's religion.

Sheftall joined with his Christian neighbors to oppose the Crown. They understood his strong feelings for independence. With their assent, he assumed command of his Parish as chairman of its Revolutionary Committee. They promptly sequestered all British property and records in the Parish.

Sheftall was later commissioned a Colonel in the Georgia Brigade. British dispatches noted that Jews, of which the Sheftall and Minis families were the most prominent, led the Georgia Rebels. They were marked for retribution. Their homes were selected for raids by Tories, who carried off their slaves and property.

The British Governor, Sir James Wright, singled Sheftall out as especially troublesome. He wrote:

"... one Sheftall, a Jew, is chairman of the Parochial Committee, as they call themselves, and this fellow issues orders to captains of vessels to depart the king's port ... And fresh insults are to be offered everyday."

Toward the end of the War, while the British still controlled Savannah, Wright recommended the arrest and expulsion of rebels. He then went on to single out special treatment for Jews: Jewish émigrés should be prevented from resettling and no new Jewish settlers should be permitted in Georgia. His explanation for such drastic measures was a tribute to colonial Jewry:

"For these people, my lord, were found to a man to have been violent rebels and persecutors of the king's loyal subjects. And however this may appear at first sight, be assured, my lord, that the times require these exertions, and without which the loyal subjects can have no peace or security in this province."

In 1777, Sheftall was appointed Commissary General of Purchases and Issues to the Georgia Militia by General Robert Howe, commanding officer of the American Forces in the Southern Department. Before the Continental Congress could approve this Federal commission, the British captured the city of Savannah in December 1778. Taken with the City were Mordecai Sheftall and other officers, including his son Sheftall Sheftall, who acted as his military aide.

When the British commander discovered that he had captured Sheftall, he placed him in a cell apart from other captured American officers. The British tried to humiliate him by placing him with slaves and drunkards. More than once, he was threatened at bayonet point. A sympathetic Hessian, who spoke German with Sheftall, supplied him with food: The British had failed to feed him for three days. Later, transferred to a prison ship, his captors made a point of providing him with pork as his main prison staple.

Sheftall recorded the trials of his imprisonment in his memoirs:

"On our way to the ...guard-house we met with Col. Campbell, who inquired of the Major who he had got there. On his naming me to him, he desired that I might be well guarded, as I was a very great rebel. The Major obeyed ... he ordered the sentry to guard me with a drawn bayonet and not to suffer me to go without reach of him ..."

Later, another officer and Sheftall had a hot argument. The officer punished him:

"... he ordered me to be confined amongst the drunken soldiers and negroes, where I suffered a great deal of abuse, and was threatened to be run through the body ... which threat he attempted to put into execution three times during the night, but was prevented by one Sergeant Campbell."

According to the customary Rules of War at the time, officers could be paroled. Sometime in March 1779, Sheftall was paroled with others to the nearby town of Sunbury. Sheftall Sheftall was not. Mordecai was clearly upset: his son was a lad, barely 16. He requested of his superiors, captured with him, that young Sheftall also be paroled. On at least two occasions, Sheftall could have escaped the British. He refused to do so because it would have meant leaving his son behind.

After much effort by Mordecai and his wife Frances, the boy was also paroled. But father and son were not yet out of the woods. Four months later, the French and Continental soldiers made an unsuccessful attempt to retake Savannah. Apparently in a panic, some English soldiers and their Tory allies threatened to kill all the parolees at Sunbury. The Sheftalls and others escaped, fleeing aboard a sailing ship bound for Charleston. But the British frigate, *"Guadeloupe"* captured them again and hauled them to the port of St. John's, Antigua, in the Caribbean. Once again, they were put on parole. The Governor of the island, however, informed them that he had no authority to engage in any prisoner exchanges.

Captives for a year, the Sheftalls were finally freed in a prisoner exchange. Returning to Savannah for revolutionaries was impossible. Their other city of choice, Charleston, was also in British hands. It was where Frances and the other Sheftall children were living. So the newly freed prisoners sailed on to Philadelphia. In this city, the war adventures of the Sheftalls would continue.

Sheftall had personally expended substantial sums of money under his military commission. In Philadelphia he, as did many others loyal to the new government, petitioned the Continental Congress for return of advances made in support of the Revolution. Generally, his pleas went unanswered. In November 1780, he again petitioned Congress without success:

"Being informed by the delegates of the state to which I belong that my application for ... pay cannot now be considered, I must intreat the Hon. Congress to have some consideration for a man who has sacrificed every thing in the cause of his country, I want nothing but justice, to be paid my advances for the public."

Despite their rebuff of Mordecai, young Sheftall Sheftall was given an important task by Congress. Would he take a ship to Charleston and, under a flag of truce deliver money and supplies to General William Moultrie and his captured troops? They needed this help badly.

He must have been an unusual young man. At the time of this approach, he was only 18 years old. He did take command of the sloop, *"Carolina Packett"* and successfully carry out his mission.

Mordecai was soon able to procure the post of purchasing agent for the state of Georgia. Father and son opened an office on Philadelphia's Front Street, not far from where Haym Salomon did business. But there was not enough work to support the Sheftall family. With such meager capital as they had available, Sheftall became a privateer. Privateering was the way governments licensed citizens to attack, harass and capture enemy shipping. The inducement for the privateer was the prize money to be gained from the raiding. Cargo and vessel sold at port could bring a fortune to a lucky raider.

Sheftall bought the schooner, *"Hetty,"* outfitting her for this special purpose. With the rest of the Sheftall family behind enemy lines in Charleston, the expenses of the *"Hetty"* mounting and the Continental Congress refusing to repay its debts to him, Mordecai must have had some serious concerns. When he was finally able to get wife and children out of Charleston, the Master of the vessel seized all their clothing to pay for their passage.

The cap on Sheftall's woes was reached when the *"Hetty"* grounded. After extensive repairs, she was back in service, only to be captured and scuttled by the British.

Returning to his home at the close of the War, Sheftall again assumed his dual role as both community and religious leader. Young Sheftall became a lawyer. It is recounted that in his later years, Sheftall Sheftall would recall his wartime adventures as one of the last survivors of the Revolutionary War in Savannah. He had by that time acquired the nickname, "Cocked Hat Sheftall." Though he was just 21 when the war ended, young Sheftall had served his country for five years as soldier and prisoner of war, as did his father.

Of the portraits presented in this book, Sheftall is the only one who resided on the frontier, away from the mainstream of early American urban Judaism. He is all the more remarkable since he was strongly religious despite his lack of regular contact with his co-religionists. There is much evidence that of the Jews living in Georgia during this period, many were under great pressure to convert or to allow the children of marriages with Christians to be raised out of the Jewish faith.

That he was an observant Jew was evident not only to him, but even to his Christian neighbors. One written invitation to him from a friend advised him that when Sheftall came to his home, the pigs would be put away and a sheep would be slaughtered for dinner. "Bring your special knife," (the knife of ritual slaughtering) the friend added.

The same staunch loyalty he had for his country he carried over to his religion. Out on the frontier when the only Jews in Savannah were the Sheftalls and the Minises, he must have hoped that more of his co-religionists would return so he could enjoy a full religious life. Each time Jews came back to Savannah to take advantage of better economic conditions, Mordecai Sheftall was there to assist with the rebirth of the community.

In 1790, Jews received equal rights as citizens of Georgia. Mordecai Sheftall, as head of the now vigorous Jewish community, was authorized to petition the governor for permission to incorporate *"Mickva Israel ... as a body politick."* Members of the congregation included Sheftall Sheftall and Levi Sheftall, Mordecai's brother, who also served as a soldier during the War.

This was not the first time Sheftall had the privilege of helping to form a new Jewish community. As a youth engaged in business, he had traveled back and forth between Savannah and Charleston on a regular basis, as had most of Savannah's Jews. In 1750, while still a teenager, he and his brother Levi helped found Charleston's Congregation Beth Elohim.

Again, while in Philadelphia in 1782, and living with other Jews who had escaped from the English occupation of New

York, Newport, Charleston and Savannah, he was among those who formally constituted Mikve Israel in that city. Among the group were well-known personages of the day, including Haym Salomon, Benjamin Nones, Michael and Bernard Gratz, Isaac DaCosta and Jonas Phillips.

As strapped as he was for money at the time, Sheftall nevertheless gave three pounds toward the erection of a synagogue. The leading contributor was the legendary Haym Salomon. Benjamin Franklin and Dr. David Rittenhouse also responded to appeals made to Christian Philadelphians for financial aid.

True to his commitment to his religion, Sheftall was an active member of this congregation. Minutes of Mikve Israel reveal that he was chosen to act as chairman on an occasion when the Parnass was accused of a conflict in arbitration proceedings.

In Savannah in July 1791, five out of 15 members present at a congregational meeting were Sheftalls. Levi was Parnass, Sheftall Sheftall was Gabay, and Benjamin Sheftall, Jr. was Secretary. Obviously, Mordecai Sheftall passed on strong Jewish feelings to his family.

Mordecai Sheftall saw no ambiguity or conflict in his love and loyalty to his religion during the Revolutionary War. His steadfastness to Judaism was equal to that love for his country.

Sheftall died in his native Georgia in 1797. He left many legacies. One of his sons, Moses, was the first American-born Jewish doctor. The Union Society, of which Mordecai was a founder, was America's first cooperative charity organization, run jointly by Protestants, Catholics and Jews. He was also an active and important Mason.

In 1825, an aging Marquis de Lafayette came to Savannah to lay the cornerstone of a monument to the Polish Revolutionary War General, Pulaski. With the cornerstone was deposited a piece of history. Inscribed upon it are the following words:

"A piece of the oaktree from Sunbury County, Georgia, under which in 1779, the charge of the Union Society was preserved, and Mr. Mordecai Sheftall, Then a prisoner of War, was elected President."

Sheftall's Savannah, c. 1700s

HAYM SALOMON

"If Mr. Haym Salomon will call upon Mr. Robert Morris tomorrow at 3:00 such business may be concluded which will be to their advantage and the advantage of their country."

Robert Morris, Sup't of Finance

He was a most unlikely patriot and hero. He did not get to America until 1772, shortly before the first shots were fired at Lexington and Concord. He was too old to bear arms and a racking cough and pain in his lungs sapped his strength. But his role during the Revolutionary War was as important and vital as that of any soldier in the field. His name was Haym Salomon.

In 1975, two centuries after he crossed the Atlantic to America, a stamp honoring Haym Salomon was issued under the series "Contributors to the Cause." The cause was the American Revolution. A legend describing Salomon's stamp reads:

"Businessman and broker Haym Salomon was responsible for raising most of the money needed to finance the American Revolution and later to save the new nation from collapse."

Most American Jews know Haym Salomon as "The Revolution's financier." It is oversimplification. He was a passionate lover of his new country, who lived less than 13 years in his adopted country after landing at New York. Of those 13 years, only five were spent in serious financial work for the Continental Congress. Had he not come to the Colonies, however, American history would have changed, and not for the better.

He is, and he deserves to be, an American legend. Much of what we know of him is legend, taken from many sources. The claims could be true or even half-true. It is certain that controversy and shadow surround his life. But while a question mark may remain concerning specifics of his accomplishments and the services he offered to his country, this is certain: he helped the Continental Congress and America's patriots. He was also loyal to his faith and gave help, financial and otherwise, as he could to Philadelphia's Jewish community. He was also a civil libertarian, in the forefront of the fight to remove Jewish civil disabilities.

Haym Salomon was a son of political strife. His hometown of Lissa, in Poland, was torched. Its Jews could no longer live there in peace. Salomon, aged 27, began an eight-year journey throughout the business centers of Europe, learning the languages of the English, the Italians and the French, which he added to his knowledge of Polish, Yiddish and German. It is certain that reports of his fluency in languages may be exaggerated. He needed the help of others to transmit Yiddish letters to his family in Europe, yet Yiddish was supposedly the language of his birth.

Wherever he traveled in Europe, Jewish merchants took a liking to him and taught him how to buy unseen merchandise and then make a profit selling it to unknown purchasers. He learned about Bills of Exchange and how to discount notes. He was in an obscure area of finance, not then commonly known. From city to city, he learned and practiced these esoteric transactions, which centuries later became commonplace. But in his own time, he was probably the American master of the bill of exchange and all of its intricacies.

Salomon was training in the world of sophisticated finance as if he were preparing for something special in the New World. And he was. He was learning how to raise money for the country across the Atlantic Ocean that he would soon adopt. In his seven remaining years, from 1778 to 1785, he helped finance the American Revolution as if by magic. For it was said that no one in the rebel colonies knew how bills of exchange worked. No one, that is, except Haym Salomon, the "Jew Broker" of Philadelphia and, perhaps, Robert Morris, who was the Superintendent of Finances for the Continental Congress.

Some historical sources have Salomon arriving in New York City in 1772; others in 1775. Whichever it was, the young Pole quickly succumbed to the Revolution's fever. He joined the Sons of Liberty, a vocal organization that marched in public, harassing the occupying British forces. He soon was assigned to hiding soldiers trapped behind the lines and assisting in their escape. He hid them in the basement of his own home. This work led to his arrest as a spy.

Salomon's imprisonment caused serious aggravation of a lung condition. His luck, however, was holding out. According to one version of the story, his ability to speak German was needed by his British captors in order for them to communicate with Hessian soldiers. But he also continued working underground for the Revolution. A letter sent to General Schuyler in 1776 verifies that an important New York leader of the Revolution vouched for Salomon's patriotism.

Captured again, he was this time sentenced to death as a spy. Gaining the confidence of a Hessian guard by speaking to him in German, Salomon was able to escape. Reports of this escape are confusing. Some say gold was offered. Another report says that the Sons of Liberty devised his escape plan. Perhaps it was they who procured the gold.

This time, Haym Salomon had to leave New York. His home and the considerable assets he had accumulated over the years were seized by the British. He sent word to his wife, Rachel, to take their children and flee to Philadelphia; he would meet them later.

Escaping to Dobbs Ferry, he had his first opportunity to see the Continental Army up close. It was an unhappy sight: soldiers were without boots or serviceable shoes, dressed in tatters, carrying outdated firearms, and foraging for food across the countryside. It was a sight he could not forget. All the way to Philadelphia from the encampment, he resolved to try to do something to help.

Philadelphia in 1778 was a busy place. Refugees from New York and other cities gathered here to escape British occupation of their cities. Jewish refugees from New York, Newport, Charleston and Savannah gathered at Mikveh Israel, the city's only Jewish congregation.

Haym Salomon began doing business at his shop on Philadelphia's Front Street, near the city's piers and docks. As he had done in New York, he was dealing in commercial paper. He petitioned the Continental Congress, informing them of his services to the government and the privations that he and his family had suffered as a result. Could they help?

"(I) was soon taken up as a spy ... by (the British General Robertson), *committed to the Provost,"* Salomon informed the Continental Congress.

"(I) was given over to the Hessian Commander ... (where I) *was of great Service to the French & American prisoners and have assisted them with money and helped them off to make their Escape ... (I) was pursued by the* (Hessian guards) *and on Tuesday the 11th inst. (I) made my happy escape from thence - ...Monsieur Demezes* (a fellow prisoner) *is now most barbarously treated at the Provost's and is seemingly in danger of*

his Life. (I) beg leave to cause him to be remembered to Congress for an Exchange.

"Your Memorialist has upon this Event most irrecoverably lost all his Effects and Credits to the Amount of Five or six thousands Pounds sterling and left his distressed Wife and a child of a month at New York waiting that they may soon have an opportunity to come out from thence with empty hands.

"In these Circumstances he most humbly prayeth to grant him any Employ in the Way of his Business whereby he may be enabled to support himself and family - Your Memorialist as in duty bound &c.

   Haym Salomon   Philad Aug 25ᵗʰ 1778"

His pleas were rejected with silence. But he was building a reputation. During the Revolutionary War, most shipping, insurance and brokering transactions in Philadelphia were carried out in a similar manner as the famous English brokers at Lloyds. Men would gather in coffee houses and insure ocean cargo, voyages and do other business on the shake of hand or on small scraps of paper.

Salomon quickly entered into the city's business life. Soon it was obvious that his knowledge of commercial instruments was outstanding. Not only was he respected for business astuteness, but for his honesty and fairness as a trader.

For all this activity, things were not good in Philadelphia. The government headquartered there had no money. The city was living with runaway inflation: a hat cost $400, shoes, $125. One silver dollar was worth $525 of greenbacks issued by the Continental Congress. The government's paper money was thrown into stoves or used for lining clothes in winter.

Salomon was resolved to do something to help. This time he wrote directly to George Washington. He would, he explained to the General, like to help some deserving patriots.

Washington took advantage of Salomon's offer and referred

them to him. Their names are a list of Revolutionary War heroes: Von Steuben, John Paul Jones, Pulaski, James Madison, Washington, and even the treasonous Benedict Arnold, while he was still a General in good standing. Salomon charged no interest for his loans.

The government could not meet its commitments. And Robert Morris, Superintendent of Finance and a master at economics himself, was unable to solve the problem. Morris went through his own considerable fortune in an effort to assist. Stubborn, proud and not well liked, he had no one to turn to for help.

By 1780, the situation was critical. Washington could no longer provide food, clothes and warmth to his Army, let alone pay them. Mutiny broke out in Connecticut and was threatening elsewhere. Washington notified Morris that the situation was desperate. Action was needed, and needed immediately.

It was said that Morris liked neither Quakers nor Jews. He had already asked Quakers for money, now he would have to go to the Jews. The name Haym Salomon was not unknown to him. General Washington and others had suggested Morris contact the Jewish broker from Philadelphia who had been helping individual patriots. Now was the time for Morris to go the "Jew Broker."

Morris could not have picked a worse time to call upon Salomon for help. He did not know it was Yom Kippur, the Day of Atonement, when he sent a messenger to fetch Haym. Haym did respond, despite the solemnity of the day.

He was then already broker to the French, Dutch and Spanish governments. Suited to his work, he would roam the docks of Philadelphia along the Delaware River, then the major seaport of the rebel government. Using his ability with languages, he would speak with sailors and ship's officers in French, German, Italian or English. He would learn from them whether or not ships still on the high seas destined for Philadelphia had a chance of delivering their cargoes safely.

Because America was at war, Europeans did not wish to send gold and silver across the Atlantic. What they sent, as evidence of their debts, were Bills of Exchange and Promissory Notes. They were made out to bearer or individual payees. Haym Salomon became informed as to whether negotiable paper had any value. He would offer to buy a merchant's note worth $500 on its face, for $460. If a merchant needed cash immediately, he would be willing to take a discount for ready payment.

Few men in America understood how Haym Salomon could turn a dollar with these transactions. But the governments of France, Holland and Spain trusted this man. Each of them named him their brokering agent in America. Later, after Morris worked with him a while, he authorized Salomon to use the title, "Broker to the Office of Finance."

In this manner Salomon received from Morris, who was by now an intimate colleague and co-worker, obligations of the Continental Congress for sale on the open market. His services were not only needed to finance the Revolution but to brace an infant Republic when the war was over. Men returning home from Revolution needed mustering out pay; pensions had to be paid out to wounded soldiers; a peacetime economy had to be steadied. He was there to help, to provide the needed funds. He was America's broker: the Broker for Freedom. And his broker's fees were substantially less than standard.

Salomon's health had been steadily declining over the years. Two imprisonments in New York worsened a lung condition that finally weakened him seriously. But before his death, he helped erect Philadelphia's first synagogue, Mikveh Israel in 1782, pledging one-quarter of its financial requirements. He was one of five Philadelphia Jews who, in 1783, petitioned the state of Pennsylvania for removal of certain civil disabilities applicable to Jews.

Salomon died in 1785, holding over $353,000 in government obligations. It is here that a controversy exists. Was he holding the government's notes as its agent or as its creditor? That sum was significant for the times. Historians seriously doubt that Salomon ever accumulated sufficient personal wealth on his own to hold such a sum against the government.

There is much evidence, through letters and otherwise, that Salomon did not begin to recoup the losses of his New York exile until 1782. That is the same year he made his large pledge to Mikveh Israel's building fund. There is, however, a letter written in 1784 in which Salomon informs his relatives in Poland that they should not send him a nephew, as they proposed. *"I do not have the means to care for him,"* he wrote back. It must have been difficult for him to admit it, this man who supported generals, politicians, Battalions and Brigades of the Continental Army.

The controversy about Salomon's real role during the Revolutionary War did not arise immediately after his death. Were the notes found in his estate really his or did they belong to the United States of America? His widow turned the notes over to a Federal official, thinking they were being inventoried. Not until 1827 did the question arise for the first time. One of Salomon's sons, also named Haym, wrote to James Madison claiming recompense for the $353,000 in negotiable paper found in the patriot's effects after his death.

His claims were denied by Congress, as were subsequent requests for redress. The issue further heated up at the turn of the 20th century, when the Federation of Polish Jews of America tried to erect a monument to his memory in New York City. There was much opposition to the proposal and a charge was made that there was no truth to the legend of Haym Salomon. German Jews opposed the memorial, alleging it was an attempt by newly arrived Polish immigrants to increase their importance.

One eminent American historian, a non-Jew, said: "The story itself is incredible ... only as an estimable merchant has he claims to any recognition."

Of what importance is it to know if the government owed this man money? For us, over 200 years later, Haym Salomon is the quintessential American; an immigrant who returned America's protection the best way he knew. He entered his country's life as a patriot, first as an activist then as financier. America was fortunate. This man with the special talents needed by the young Republic at that time was available and willing to help.

His concerns did not end with America. He fostered his religion and petitioned his government when he thought it was treating him unjustly because he was a Jew. Was it significant that his country made a call for his services on the day he considered most holy?

Along with 800 citizens of Philadelphia, Haym Salomon signed a petition addressed to President George Washington and the United States Congress in 1783, pledging their support for the New American government. The following year, Salomon, Gershom Seixas (the patriot rabbi), Simon Nathan, Asher Meyers and Bernard Gratz refused to accept a Pennsylvania statute that required a belief in the New Testament as a requirement to hold public office. They reminded the legislature that Jews also had a hand as patriots in the founding of the United States:

"Your memorialists beg farther to represent, that in the religious books of the Jews, which are or may be in every man's hands, there are no such doctrines or principles established, as are inconsistent with the safety and happiness of the People of Pennsylvania, and that the conduct and behavior of the Jews in this and the neighbouring states, has always tallied with the great design of the revolution; that the Jews of Charleston, New York, New-Port and other posts, occupied by the British ... have suffered for their attachment to the Revolution ... The Jews of Pennsylvania in proportion to the number of their members,

can count with any religious society whatsoever ... they have served in the continental army; some went out in the militia to fight the common enemy; all of them have cheerfully contributed to the support of the militia, and of this state...

"(We) humbly pray, that if your honours, from any other consideration than the subject of this address, should think proper to call a convention for revising the constitution, you would be pleased to recommend this to the notice of that convention."

America has not forgotten Haym Salomon. In Chicago, he stands in a statue with George Washington and Robert Morris, these three heroes of America's Revolution memorialized in bronze. Six American presidents have recalled his contribution while honoring him. A Liberty Ship named for him served with distinction during World War II.

Lorado Taft sculpture of George Washington, Haym Salomon, Robert Morris, City of Chicago

THOMAS KENNEDY *

"There is only one opponent that I fear at this time, and that is prejudice - our prejudices..."

Thomas Kennedy

The legislator sat back on his bench and folded his arms high over his chest. The dark hair combed forward over his forehead, set off his lean face. The look on his face was impassive, and he stared straight ahead. Today his bill was again coming up before the Maryland legislature. He knew it would be defeated, as it had been before.

"Kennedy's Jew baby," one of his fellow legislators shouted across the chamber of the Maryland House of Delegates, pointing a finger at him. The man shifted in his seat, his face showing no emotion. Thomas Kennedy, Representative of Washington County to the Maryland Legislature, was committed to a legal battle that could not possibly bring him any political advantage.

* Thomas Kennedy is the only non-Jew in this book. He is included because of his important contribution to religious freedom in America.

Born in Scotland in 1776, Kennedy migrated with his family to the United States in 1796. They settled in Western Maryland. Politically astute, Kennedy was elected to the State Legislature. Kennedy was Presbyterian and had no Jews in his district. Nor was he personally acquainted with any. But he had a strong feeling about the inequality with which the State of Maryland disenfranchised all non-Christians. As a Jeffersonian, he had a burning desire to change the law.

In 1818, when Kennedy took his seat representing Washington County, no person could hold public office, sit on a jury, practice law, or command a militia in the State of Maryland unless he took an oath only Christians were able to subscribe to. The law disqualified not only Jews, but "atheists and infidels" as well. It was so written in the Maryland Constitution. It was directly opposed to the United States Constitution, which guaranteed all Americans the right to practice religion or not, as they saw fit. But in 1818, the Federal government was not as concerned with civil rights as it is today, since the guarantee was federal and did not apply to the states.

The contradiction was absurd. Baltimorean Simon T. Levy became a national hero at the battle of Fallen Timbers during the Indian Wars. He fought beside Andrew Jackson and received a Federal appointment to the first graduating class of West Point.

Upon graduation, Levy was an American army officer and could take command at any U.S. Army post. He could serve his country as it had trained him to do. But Levy could not serve in the Maryland Militia, his state's home guard, because his oath would be invalid.

Kennedy was not the first to concern himself with the inequality of the law. Solomon Etting, a Baltimore Jew, petitioned the legislature for removal of these humiliating civil disabilities in 1797. The petition was never acted upon and, in time, was lost in the legislative hopper, The bill came up for consideration again in 1802 and was voted down in 1804 once more. Forgotten again for a dozen more years, the bill surfaced in 1816 and was dismissed with no action at all.

When similar petitions were made in other states, they were acted upon favorably within a few years. During elections for the New York State Assembly in 1737, Adolph Philipse lost his seat because the Assembly held a Jew was not qualified for election. The principle never rose again; no one ever used it against any Jew and the matter disappeared. The New York State Constitution of 1777 settled the issue by eliminating all religious qualifications for office holders.

By 1818, Thomas Kennedy assumed the responsibility to oversee the repeal of Maryland's unjust law. In the same year, Maryland was home to no more than 150 Jews. Most lived in Baltimore. There was no political advantage to be gained for this legislator from the West. Kennedy approached his task with steadfastness seldom seen in American politics and for an unselfish goal.

Would Thomas Kennedy have persevered, knowing his bill would be defeated time after time, year after year, for eight years? That he would be defeated for re-election by his opponents who called his slate the "Jew Ticket"? That his bill would be called "Kennedy's Jew Baby"? That he would be vilified by his political opponents? The answer is probably "yes."

Kennedy not only had nothing to gain politically or otherwise, he never even consulted with any Jews about what he intended to do. He acted out of genuine concern for the civil rights and equality of a tiny group of Marylanders, none of whom he represented, none of whom he even knew. He did, however, understand the injustice of denying minority groups within a society, the privileges the majority enjoyed. One writer advances the idea that Kennedy was able to transcend his family's rock-ribbed prejudices to become a total and complete egalitarian.

At first, Kennedy's job seemed simple. He requested and was made chairman of a committee to consider an appropriate bill. Two other legislators, both Baltimoreans, were also appointed. Judge Henry Brackenridge and Ebenezer S. Thomas were not only sympathetic with Kennedy's aims, they had Jewish friends and understood their concern with the disabilities under which they lived. Solomon Cohen and Jacob Etting assisted Thomas, Brackenridge and others with information and statistics needed to make the bill a success.

Unfortunately, Maryland's Jews realized that eliminating all disabilities for everyone was not a practical goal. They knew attacking the oath on behalf of Jews alone was a safer road. It would be well into the 20th century before a general law to remove all civil disabilities would be passed in Maryland. In fact, the Blasphemy Act of 1924 still drew a six-month prison sentence and a $100 fine for anyone who denied the divinity of Christ and the Holy Trinity.

Such disability laws were not new to Maryland. On February 23, 1658, Maryland's first Jewish settler, Dr. Jacob Lumbrozo, was charged with violating the Toleration Act, as it was ironically called. The law required all citizens of Maryland to accept "the doctrine of the Trinity." The breach carried with it death or loss of all property. Lumbrozo was spared a trial when Richard Cromwell, at that time Lord Protector of the Commonwealth of England, ordered a general amnesty.

Dr. Lumbrozo was set free. He continued to live in the colony, surely with great care not to make public his religious beliefs.

On Kennedy's bill's first vote, taken in 1819, the Conservatives won the day. It was defeated. So Kennedy dug in. He was not happy with the wording of his bill. Idealist that he was, he sought to eliminate all civil disabilities, not just those of the Jews, but "atheists and infidels" as well. For now, he would have to settle for the Jews alone. At least everyone agreed that Jews believed, as did Christians, that there was a future state of "rewards and punishments." That was part of the oath that was required by the state of Maryland. Atheists and infidels could not take such an oath.

Kennedy's bill then took on the unpleasant name of the "Jew Bill" the same name as the bill that had appeared before England's Parliament in a similar fight waged in 1753. The English battle for Jewish equality took longer than America's; it was not until 1858 that any Jew could take a seat in Parliament. England's oath of office was more stringent than Maryland's. In addition to Jews, Catholics and all other dissenters from the Anglican Church were disqualified from holding office and attaining other civic privileges.

By 1847, these English disabilities began to fall through laws passed by the British Parliament. In the same year, however, Lionel de Rothschild, English head of the powerful House of Rothschild, was elected to Parliament. The members refused to seat him because he was a Jew. Every election until 1858 saw Rothschild reelected to Parliament from the Borough of London, and every election he was rejected by the Parliament. The city of London, which had four seats in Parliament, was to be underrepresented for almost 10 years!

In Maryland, Kennedy was to acquire a new ally outside the state legislature: the press. Lines were drawn in a battle that reached into all of the United States and across the Atlantic to Europe. He was blunt and open about what he felt was wrong about Maryland's religious laws. In 1822, Kennedy addressed his fellow legislators:

"Religious liberty does not exist in Maryland, for religious liberty cannot be said to exist under any government where men are not permitted to worship God in the manner most agreeable to the dictates of their own consciences, or what is the same thing, denied the enjoyment of civil rights, and rendered incapable of holding any office, civil, military or judicial, except that they acknowledge their belief in a particular system of religion.

" ... when the immortal Washington and his illustrious com-
peers, selected from every state in the Union, met in convention
to frame a constitution ... they unanimously declared that 'no
religious test shall ever be required as a qualification to any
office or public trust under the United States.' Such a declaration, at such a time, and from such an assemblage ... calls loud-
ly for our admiration; they broke the last link of religious tyran-
ny, and put an end to the dominion of superstition... "

Despite his eloquence and logic, the bill was defeated.

After more defeats in the legislature, Kennedy tried to temper his "Jew Bill" by filing a broader one eliminating the word
'Jew' and including all non-Christians. He called it "An Act to
extend to the Citizens of Maryland the same civil rights and
privileges that are enjoyed under the Constitution of the United
States." That, too, was defeated.

Kennedy's bill now was the means by which opposing parties in Maryland sought to gain political control of the state. It
seemed no one really cared about the bill, but only the struggle
for power that it represented. And one of the first orders of the
day was to get rid of Kennedy. During the 1823 elections
Kennedy ran against Benjamin Calloway. It was an ugly campaign that focused on the "Jew Bill" and Judaism, though not
one Jew lived in the district.

Kennedy was called "an enemy of Christianity," his slate
was called the "Jew ticket." He was accused of "being half-Jew
and the other half not-Christian." And of being a "Judas
Iscariot."

Kennedy was defeated, but not daunted. At the next election, he had another powerful ally: public opinion came to his
quiet agrarian community and was solidly for Kennedy, as were
more of his fellow legislators. He was re-elected. When he
returned to the House, he spoke with great eloquence once
again, in defense of his bill:

"I am free to declare that if Christianity cannot stand without the aid of persecution ... let it fall; and let a new system, more rational and more benevolent, take its place."

On February 26, 1825, the "Jew Bill" finally passed, winning by a one-vote margin, 26 to 25. To their shame, one-third of the legislators absented themselves on that day so they need not have voted. The rules of the House of Delegates required that a bill be voted twice, passing both times. On January 5, 1826, the law was finally confirmed and enacted by a more robust vote of 45 to 33.

During the eight-year struggle to enact his bill, Kennedy was transformed from a little known and obscure legislator to a man of stature. His addresses to the Maryland legislature were published in American newspapers and circulated throughout the United States. They were presented to members of Parliament and other interested persons in England. They were also translated into German and Hebrew.

Kennedy's courage and his exciting fight received much notoriety. The length of time that passed before the successful enactment of the "Jew Bill" kept him before the American public for years. Yet this important chapter in American history and the country's innate genius for fairness and justice, has been pushed into a corner. No historian has made an in-depth study of Kennedy and his remarkable fight against the army of bigots massed against him. It is a story waiting to be told, for there is much drama and a lesson for all Americans to learn.

The American press, the Catholics of Maryland and the religious community in general, recognized an injustice had come to an end. They were pleased to learn of its demise. The American public seemed to have more sense than did some of their elected representatives.

The battle to remove civil disabilities for Jews did not end in Maryland. The states of Rhode Island and North Carolina would maintain similar laws until 1842 and 1868 respectively.

But in no state did a legislator such as Thomas Kennedy emerge to champion Jews. In no state did the battle turn as ugly and bitter as it did in Maryland. And in no state did the public receive so much information about the legislative process. The passage of the equality bill was protracted and loaded with political struggle for the state of Maryland. It was not only a great monument for Thomas Kennedy, who pushed it through despite great odds; it is the affirmation of the equality of all Americans before the law. That was what Kennedy understood. Jews represented to him the disenfranchised of the moment. It is unfortunate that Blacks were not seen in the same way. Perhaps America's bloodiest war could have been avoided.

There is a plaque dedicated to the memory of Thomas Kennedy at Sinai Hospital in Baltimore, the hospital founded by the Jewish community of the city. After detailing his political career, a quote is inscribed at the base of the plaque. It says:

"I PRAY I MAY DIE BEFORE I CEASE TO BE THE FRIEND OF CIVIL AND RELIGIOUS LIBERTY, AND A SUPPORTER OF THE RIGHTS OF THE PEOPLE."

The citizens of Washington County of the State of Maryland were privileged to be represented by a special and courageous legislator. Their votes sent a man to the legislature who would forever erase a civil injustice in their state.

Perhaps the greatest tribute to Kennedy occurred soon after the final passage of "the Jew Bill." Several months later, both Solomon Etting and Jacob Cohen were elected to the Baltimore City Council. They took their seats as equals with other Councilmen ... after taking the amended oath Kennedy worked so hard to secure for them and those who followed.

Portrait of Thomas Kennedy, the Western Maryland Room, Washington County Free Library, Hagerstown, Maryland

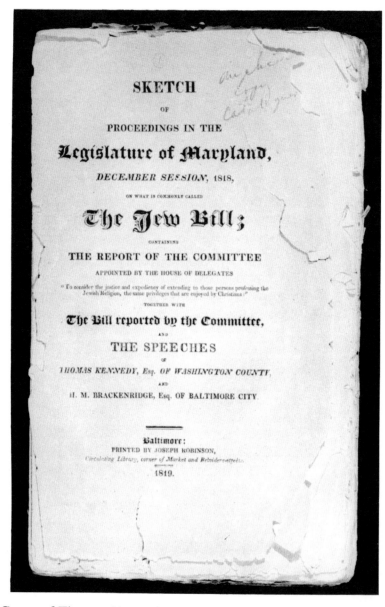

Cover of Thomas Kennedy's "The Jew Bill, " Jewish Museum of Maryland

"An Act for the relief of the Jews in Maryland".

Be it enacted by the General Assembly of Maryland that every Citizen of this State professing the Jewish Religion, and who shall hereafter be appointed to any Office or public trust under the State of Maryland, shall in addition to the oaths required to be taken by the Constitution and Laws of the State, or of the United States make and subscribe a declaration of his belief in a future State of Rewards and Punishments, in the stead of the declaration now required by the Constitution and form of Government of this State.

And be it enacted, That the several clauses and sections of the declaration of rights, Constitution and form of Government and every part of any law of this State contrary to the provisions of this act so far as respects the sect of people aforesaid, shall be and the same is hereby declared to be repealed and annulled, on the confirmation hereof.

And be it enacted, That if this act shall be confirmed by the General Assembly of Maryland after the next election of Delegates in the first Session after such new election as the Constitution and form of Government directs, in such case this Act and the alterations of the said Constitution and form of Government shall constitute and be valid as a part of the said Constitution and form of Government to all intents and purposes any thing therein contained to the Contrary notwithstanding.

Handwritten page from "The Jew Bill," Jewish Museum of Maryland

URIAH PHILLIPS LEVY

*"I would rather be a cabin boy in the United States Navy
than hold the rank of admiral in any other service."*

Uriah Phillips Levy

On April 12, 1861, the day the Civil War began, aging
Commodore Uriah Phillips Levy was the United States Navy's
highest-ranking officer. He had begun his 60-year sailing career
as a cabin boy on a commercial sailing ship in 1802 and fought
his way through the ranks. Along the way, he acquired a reputation as a hot-tempered firebrand and a troublemaker.

During half-a-century of military service to his country,
Levy survived six courts-martial, two Boards of Inquiry, multi-
ple duels and countless personal confrontations with spiteful
fellow officers. Twice, he was expelled from the U.S. Navy. As
a young sailor, he was impressed into an English Navy work
gang and for 16 months was in a British military prison after his
capture during the War of 1812.

Levy spent much of his life defending his right to be a
Jewish naval officer and a patriot. Most of the problems he
faced in the U.S. Navy arose from his dedication to his religion
and his refusal to accept insults directed at it.

Today, his portrait hangs prominently at the U.S. Naval Academy's museum at Annapolis, Maryland. There he is, standing tall, a scroll in his hand proclaiming: *"Author of the Abolition of Flogging in the Navy of the United States."*

Uriah Phillips Levy was born in Philadelphia in 1792. His life reads like fiction: it is packed with improbable events. Late 18th century Philadelphia was one of America's great seaports. Young Uriah lived just a few blocks from its busy piers, just off Front Street on Elfreth's Alley. The synagogue was a few blocks away, on Cherry Street, and he attended services regularly with the rest of his family.

(Elfreth's Alley is today America's oldest continuously occupied residential street. Highway I95 separates the street from the docks and wharves on the Delaware River, now known as Penn's Landing.)

Fired by his love for the sea - his boyhood hero was John Paul Jones - he scampered along the piers of the Delaware River, admiring its sailing ships and envying the sailors who shipped out to sea aboard their planked decks.

Levy's love for America came from his grandfather, Jonas Phillips, who fought with the Continental Army during the Revolutionary War. Phillips was also the first president of Mikveh Israel, Philadelphia's first synagogue and America's fourth oldest. On his mother's side, Levy was descended from Spanish and Portuguese Jews, one of whom was physician to the royal court. He was proud of his ancestors.

When he was just 10, Levy learned that a cabin boy on the coaster schooner, *"New Jerusalem"* had fallen ill. He applied for the job. With a promised salary of $4 a month and assurances from the ship's Master, a Quaker, that he would be released in two years to study for and become Bar Mitzvah, he left for sea without telling his family. As he was later to remark, *"I have more than the usual amount of salt water in my veins."* He was passionate about the sea and its rough way of life.

* * * * *

His two years of indenture completed, Levy returned to Philadelphia to study for his Bar Mitzvah. His parents arranged for a Dutch Jew to instruct him. The teacher was also a ship's chandler, so the young boy studied tradewinds as well as Torah. On the day of his Bar Mitzvah, after completing his portion, he made an announcement: *"I intend to return to sea,"* he said, *"and as soon as possible."*

His mother and father did everything they could to dissuade him, without success. The smell of tar on mooring lines and brine in the sea air was too strong a pull for the boy. He was allowed to return to his world of sailing ships.

After another apprenticeship, Levy came ashore again, this time to enroll in a maritime training school in Philadelphia. There, he learned the skills of navigation, map reading, and cargo handling. Upon completion, he qualified as a Second Mate. Though barely 17, he had already acquired a reputation as a fine seaman. Levy quickly landed a position aboard a commercial sailing ship, beginning his career in the Merchant Marine.

In the years following the Revolutionary War, the British Navy roamed the North Atlantic with little opposition. Her mighty ships of the line needed great amounts of manpower. Unable to recruit men voluntarily, England began the practice of impressing American seamen into naval service. It assumed the position that legally, most Americans were British since they were born in the Colonies before the Revolutionary War. "Once British, always British," was the motto of the impressment gangs. That Americans had fought - and won - a war to gain independence from the English King was of no consequence to the British Navy.

Calling at the island of Tortola in the British Virgin Islands, Levy was caught up in the impressment net. The leader of the kidnap gang, a Royal Marine, made an insulting remark about

Jews. Levy punched him square on the chin, receiving a rifle butt on his skull in return. It was the first of a long series of fights he would be involved in throughout his life. When he awoke, he found himself in the well of a rowboat, on his way to service aboard one of His Britannic Majesty's Men-O'-War.

Fortunately for the young Second Mate, he still retained his officer's papers. After two weeks of impressment as an ordinary seaman, he was able to convince a high-ranking officer that he was an American citizen born after the Revolution, and a qualified merchant seaman. The "Yankee Jew," as he was known aboard ship, was turned ashore at Kingston, Jamaica. He made his way back to Philadelphia via Boston.

Back to sea at the age of 19, Uriah Phillips Levy became Master of the schooner, *"George Washington."* He promptly nailed a *mezzuzah* to the frame of the Captain's cabin.

By 1812, America and England were at war again. Although Levy was beginning a career at sea and it was apparent that he would become successful as a captain, he was also anxious to serve his country. Levy applied for and received the rank of Sailing Master aboard a U.S. Navy warship.

Later, Levy volunteered to serve with the legendary American raider ship, *"Argus."* She was the first American warship to penetrate English waters during the War of 1812. After one of the raids, the Captain of the *"Argus"* left a prize ship in Uriah's care, instructing him to sail her to a French port. On his way, Levy was captured by a British Sloop, which took him in tow. He finally wound up a prisoner-of-war for 16 months, at the infamous Dartmoor Prison. Despite his imprisonment, he never forgot his religion and tried to organize services among the Jewish prisoners.

Returning to America at war's end, Levy resolved to make the Navy his career. The legend of the tempestuous Jewish-American naval officer was about to begin.

At a time when there was no Naval Academy (the Annapolis academy was not founded until 1845), future officers were plucked from America's upper class to serve aboard vessels as Midshipmen. There was a definite class system in operation, and Uriah Phillips Levy was of the wrong class. The Midshipman's classrooms were the ships of the line. It was from the decks of these ships that the United States Navy reaped its harvest of officers.

Determined to prove that Jews could also serve their country, Levy made an important observation that would have great significance for minority aspirants to naval service:

"What will be the future of our navy if others such as I refuse to serve because of the prejudice of a few? There will be other Hebrews in times to come, of whom America will have need. By serving myself, I will help give them a chance to serve."

Levy was giving the world notice that he planned on making the U.S. Navy his home.

His words were prophetic: his persistence did make way for others of his faith. Aside from the many Jewish officers who would later attend Annapolis or rise through the ranks, Levy's words seem to have been particularly appropriate for one of his distant kinsmen, the family of Raphael Jacob Moses, who served as a Major with the Confederate Army.

Moses' son, Raphael, Jr., entered the Naval Academy at Annapolis in 1860, but resigned in 1861 to fight with the Confederate Navy as a Midshipman. From 1890 to 1930, eight grand- or great-grandsons of Raphael Jacob Moses attended the U.S. Naval Academy. Seven retired as senior officers, the eighth left Annapolis for medical reasons.

Levy showed the way for others who would follow him - but at a price. The worst indignities would first have to be suffered by this determined young man who refused to deny his religion. He would fuse his patriotism, profession and religion into a life's passion.

As determined as Levy was to serve, others were just as dedicated to encouraging his failure. He was posted as Sailing Master aboard the *"Franklin"* and the long road of prejudice, treatment as a social outcast, silence, humiliation and trumped-up military trials would begin.

At a dance in Philadelphia at which the officers and Midshipmen of the *"Franklin"* were in attendance, one of his Lieutenants called him a "damned Jew." The insult ended in a call to duel. On the field of honor, the Lieutenant fired at and missed Uriah four times. Each time, Uriah purposely fired over the head of his adversary, intending to miss. Finally, the angry and frustrated officer shouted out, "I mean to kill you." His final shot following, slicing at one of Levy's ears. Uriah's supporters urged him to aim true and hit his opponent. He did, killing the Lieutenant.

The Navy took no action. But in Philadelphia, he was charged by the city with the crime of issuing a challenge to duel. He was acquitted, but not before his dead opponent's cousin challenged him to another duel. The Master of the *"Franklin"* expressly forbid any acceptance of the challenge. Then, when Levy returned to the *"Franklin,"* another officer called him a "damned Jew." This affair ended in a court-martial for both, each receiving a reprimand.

Despite these problems, on March 5, 1817, 15 years after a 10-year old cabin boy ran away to sea, Uriah Phillips Levy was commissioned a Lieutenant in the U.S. Navy. It was an age when ships were powered by wind on sail and the strong backs of sailors working in unison; when Masters sailed by the positions of heavenly bodies; and when sea charts were unreliable. Yet Levy was an unusually skillful sailor who could manage seamen well and steer his ship through all manner of uncertainty.

Attaining officer's rank did not improve his relations with his fellow officers, however. Levy had a large ego and could at times be pompous. Assigned to the frigate *"United States,"* his

Captain expressed displeasure at the posting and refused to admit him aboard. Overruled by a superior officer, the Captain still required the order to be given twice. This time, the Commodore of the fleet became irate and ordered the Captain to accept his new Lieutenant aboard ship as posted by the Navy.

At the time, and until the Civil War, Commodore was the highest rank in the Navy, there was no designation of Admiral. Commodore was the rank that Levy himself would eventually attain.

Levy assumed his new post to the obvious distaste of most officers aboard ship. Space was at a premium on a sailing ship. The Ward Room was usually the only place where officers could gather socially for small talk and coffee. The Officer's Mess was where officers took their meals together with the Captain. There, away from their rigorous sea watches, they could banter and establish friendships. Often during his career, Levy was not permitted to be a part of that social interaction. Ostracized, it must have been difficult for him to take meals in a room where others ignored his presence or, worse, made nasty remarks about him or his religion. The officers soon changed their minds, after watching him perform his duties. They realized he was an excellent sailor.

While aboard the *"United States,"* Uriah was to witness his first flogging. He knew about the practice only academically. At maritime school in Philadelphia, students were taught that it was accepted as the only way to maintain discipline aboard ship. After his graduation, while sailing in the merchant navy, he saw many seamen whose backs were raised with permanent, purple welts from a lashing with a cat-o'-nine-tails. He resolved that when his time came to command a ship, he would never use the whip to enforce discipline, or as a means to punish his sailors.

By 1845, Levy began writing articles in national magazines not only campaigning against flogging, but against supplying rum rations to seamen and ordering forced attendance at religious services. He worked with Senators and Congressmen to advise an unaware American public of these abuses. His cousin, Mordecai Manuel Noah, featured Uriah's articles in his newspapers and even edited them for readability.

As a result of Levy's efforts, the use of flogging was severely limited by legislation in 1850 and again in 1852. By 1862, it was outlawed entirely. Grog rations aboard ship was banned in 1852.

Proud of his part in the demise of the lash, Levy ordered the following inscription carved on his tombstone:

"Father of the law for the Abolition of the barbarous practice of corporal punishment in the Navy of the United States."

The inscription was part of Levy's bravado. He needed others to help him: Noah to put his thoughts into good words and New Hampshire Senator John P. Hale, who argued long and often in the Senate with Levy's help, to eventually pass the law abolishing flogging.

But before he could reach the respected position of Naval Reformer, he had to travel over rough seas. The young officer continued to parry anti-Jewish remarks. He endured more courts-martial by his spiteful enemies. He defended each one personally, but would lose them all. His fellow officers meted out harsh punishment, but each time a higher authority, sometimes the President of the United States himself, softened the punishment or eliminated it altogether.

Twice, shipboard courts-martial cashiered him from the Navy; both times the President of the United States overruled the offending officers. It was generally felt that while Levy was a hothead and even pompous, he was a topnotch sailor. His superiors were watching him and knew he was under great pressure from snobbish officers who wished to keep the Navy the private preserve of the Christian upper class.

To the credit of the Navy, most of its top officers backed

Levy in his struggle to succeed. They were also aware of the prejudice directed at him. Uriah Levy may have been having problems with lower-echelon officers who were constantly sniping at him, but he could count upon the fairness and protection of the top brass, when it counted.

Not only was the young officer battling with his colleagues, he became engaged in international incidents as well. Once, he forced a French Captain to apologize for rude anti-Semitic remarks made after a near collision at sea. The haughty Frenchman backed down when he realized that Levy was prepared to board his ship with a contingent of armed marines.

In Brazil, while serving on a frigate making a call to that country, he and a shipmate rushed to the aid of an American seaman who was being kidnapped by Brazilian sailors on the docks of Rio de Janeiro. Levy received a bad hand wound in the fray. When more of his shipmates came to their aid, the Brazilians quickly retired.

The next day, the Royal Barge pulled alongside the American frigate. Its passenger, the Emperor of Brazil, asked to see the American officer who so bravely defended a common seaman. "You have my congratulations and compliments," said Emperor Dom Pedro I. They spoke in French. So impressed was Dom Pedro with Uriah, that he pointed to a huge 60-gun Man O' War. "I would like to offer you the Captaincy of that ship. It is the highest rank in my navy, after Admiral."

The offer carried with it some irony. A descendant of Portuguese royalty was offering a descendant of expelled Portuguese Jews a high position in his government.

Levy's response, which was reported back to his shipmates by officers present during the conversation, was *"I would rather be a cabin boy in the United States Navy than hold the rank of Admiral in any other service."* When word of this statement got back to the ship, his popularity soared - until the next scrap.

Another important point in his career occurred in 1857.

After a lifetime of service in which there were periods when he was stricken from the active list for economic reasons, he attained the high and important rank of Captain. As with everything else, he won this rank only after a struggle.

In 1855, Levy and 200 other naval officers were dismissed from the Navy "for the efficiency of the service. The "efficiency" was a paring of elderly officers for economic reasons. Levy and others requested a hearing. A Court of Inquiry was set up.

As he had done so often before, Levy prepared his own defense. But this time, he had the backup of noted attorney Benjamin F. Butler, a former Attorney General and Secretary of War. Butler arranged a massive production of witnesses, which included 22 officers and ex-officers. In addition, a full array of distinguished Americans appeared, which included the president of a New York bank, the Mayor of Washington, D.C., a poet, former Congressmen and Senators, the Collector of Customs for New York City and the Governor of New Jersey. In all, 53 witnesses testified in Levy's favor.

Then, Levy made an address to the Board on his own. It took four days to complete the argument, reading from over 100 pages. Every American, regardless of his religious beliefs, should read it. In it, he traced his career, complete with the suffering and indignities he was forced to endure because he was a Jew.

"My parents were Israelites," he informed the Board. *"I was nurtured in the faith of my ancestors. In deciding to adhere to it, I have but exercised a right, guaranteed to me by the Constitution of my native State, and of the United States - a right given to all men by their Maker - a right more precious to each of us than life itself...*

"I have to complain - more in sorrow than in anger do I say it - that in my official experience I have with little to encourage, though with much frustrate ... At an early day, and especially when it became known to the officers of my age and grade, that

I aspired to the lieutenancy, and still more, after I had gained it, I was forced to encounter a large share of the prejudice and hostility by which for so many ages, the Jew has been pursued...

" Never ... was there a man, in the ranks of our profession, against whom, in the breasts of certain members of that profession, prejudices so unjust and yet so strong, have so long and so incessantly rankled."

As a result of Levy's passionate presentation, the Board of Inquiry reinstated him. He volunteered his services to President Lincoln at the outbreak of the Civil War. He was too old and Lincoln politely declined the offer. However, the President observed drolly, since the Commodore had such extensive experience with military justice, his expertise would be put to good use. He was assigned to the Board of Military Justice.

On March 22, 1862, Uriah Phillips Levy succumbed to pneumonia. His funeral procession began at New York's Spanish and Portuguese synagogue, marching with full Naval honors down Broadway. Senior officers, flanked by marching sailors and marines, carried the coffin of the Navy's most controversial officer. The United States Navy had at last honored its most troublesome officer.

Aside from the controversies Levy had caused among his colleagues during his years in the Navy, many Jews were not happy with the notoriety he received as a result of his pinpointing anti-Semitism in the service. He ignored their complaints in the same way he parried anti-Jewish remarks.

What makes Uriah Phillips Levy so important is his genuine devotion to the three things that meant the most to him: his profession, his country and his religion. He insisted on the right to practice his faith even when he was the only Jew aboard ship. It would have been easier for him to ignore his religion or not be sensitive about it. That he refused to do.

Levy was a lifelong member of New York's Spanish and

Portuguese synagogue. He was active in establishing religious schools for other synagogues. He was a founder of the first synagogue in the District of Columbia. When he was Commander of America's Naval Squadron in the Mediterranean, he brought back earth from Palestine to be placed in Jewish graves during burials. He never hid nor denied his Jewishness, even when it would have spared him grief.

As a patriot, he worked to abolish flogging and restore dignity to the sailor's craft. Later in life, he acquired another hero, Thomas Jefferson. He bought Monticello, Jefferson's crumbling estate. Levy had become a wealthy man from good real estate investments in a growing New York City. He used some of this wealth not to buy Monticello for himself, but to restore it so all Americans might see how one of their great presidents once lived.

When the Civil War started, the South requisitioned the property. After the war, it was returned to Levy's heirs, who had to restore it once again.

Levy insisted on sailing for his country when he could have earned a fortune as a Master in the merchant marine. When he left the *"George Washington"* to serve in the War of 1812 at the age of 19, he was not only ship's Master, but also its half owner. It must have been a lonely road. Often the object of scorn from his fellow officers, Levy had no place to turn for help. He had to resolve all the indignities in the middle of a lonely sea. The combination of his ability, talent as a sailor and perseverance helped to open the door for others to follow with less pain.

Levy understood the prejudicial force martialed against him because of his religion. With this ability, he was able to say:

"...are American Christians now to begin the persecution of the Jews? Of the Jews who stand among them the representatives of the patriarchs and the prophets; - the Jews to whom were committed the oracles of God; - the Jews from whom came the founder of Christianity; ...

"What is my case today, if you yield to this injustice, may to-morrow be that of the Roman Catholic or the Unitarian; the Episcopalian or the Methodist; the Presbyterian or the Baptist. There is but one safeguard .. an honest, whole hearted, inflexible support of the Constitution."

Levy was not the only Jewish naval officer at the time. He was, however, the only one to stick it out. His brother Jonas sailed in command of a vessel during the Mexican-American War. But Jonas retired from naval service. Levi Charles Harby, a fellow prisoner with Uriah at Dartmoor, served as an officer during the War of 1812. Harby also retired from the Navy to serve as officer aboard a Customs Cutter.

Then there was the fantastic, diminutive John Ordraneaux. Born in France, Ordraneaux graduated from the Naval Academy at Bordeaux. He emigrated to America after being granted Letters of Marque by Congress so that he could operate as a Privateer, raiding British shipping during the War of 1812. Ordraneaux coaxed the Jews of Philadelphia into giving him funds to outfit a ship. Then he stalked the waterfronts of the Delaware River and Chesapeake Bay for a crew.

He was a thorn in British flesh, bringing in prizes exceeding millions of dollars. His Baltimore Clipper, *"Prince of Neuchaftel,"* was crewed by 36 men. It fought the British *"Endymion"* in a heroic battle. Ordraneaux bested an opposing crew five times the size of his own. He spurred his own men on by threatening to blow up their Clipper if they surrendered. When the fight was over, only eight of his crew remained alive. This doughty Jew, his face pitted with smallpox scars, was characterized by one of his men as *"a Jew by persuasion, a Frenchman by birth, an American for convenience and diminutive in stature."*

But Harby, Jonas Levy and the fearless Ordraneaux all left American naval service to pursue other professions. Only Uriah Levy among them resolved to remain in the Navy and make it a career. He must have been an example to his younger brothers, Morton and Benjamin, who followed him as officers in the merchant navy.

He did that and more: he helped make naval service possible for all Americans, not just the Christian elite.

Both his gravestone in New York and portrait at Annapolis declare the role of this man who helped abolish the use of the lash aboard American ships. That deed alone is sufficient for any person's life work. Levy was justifiably proud of the part he played in ending brutality aboard American ships.

The best definition of whom and what he was came from Levy himself. Characterizing his life, he once said, *"I am a Sailor, an American and a Jew."*

The *"U.S.S. Levy,"* a destroyer escort, was launched in Port Newark, New Jersey on March 28, 1943 in Uriah Phillips Levy's honor. He would have been proud of the ship named for him. The *"U.S.S. Levy"* was well known as a determined submarine hunter during the Second World War.

On December 13, 1959, the United States Navy recognized Levy's love for his Navy, country and religion. The Jewish chapel at Norfolk, Virginia's Naval Station was dedicated in his honor. "May his eager, ardent and magnetic personality hover in this chapel and draw you closer together as you worship Almighty God and serve the country he loved so well," said the Admiral at the dedication ceremony.

Commodore Uriah Phillips Levy, U.S. Naval Academy Museum, Annapolis, Maryland

SOLOMON NUÑES CARVALHO

"He was a success in all of his lives: as portraitist, photographer, explorer, historian, inventor and Jewish community leader."

Biographer Joan Sturhan

At the turn of the 18th Century, Charleston, South Carolina was one of America's largest and most important cities. It was also one of its loveliest. Warm breezes, sweeping up from the South Atlantic, gave birth to a semi-tropical economy fueled by slavery and sugar. West Indian trade shaped Charleston's style of life, architecture, manners and society.

Over 600 Jews lived in Charleston. They enjoyed a reputation of wealth and culture in what was at that time North America's largest Jewish city. Architecturally, Charleston was somewhere between British Colonial and Caribbean. Palmettos added to the exotic charm of this city on the Atlantic Ocean, located at the confluence of the Ashley and Cooper Rivers.

Many of Charleston's Jews shared family names with their West Indian cousins. They sailed back and forth to the lush tropical islands, trading with their relatives, and sometimes stayed in the islands for periods of time, to work, to marry, or to begin an apprenticeship in a family business. But Charleston was their home.

It was in this dynamic and exciting city that Solomon Nuñes Carvalho was born in 1815.

This was the era of a combined Canadian and U.S. Jewish population of approximately 2,500. Charleston's large Jewish community wielded an influence on the rest of American Jewry. It was in Charleston that young Judah P. Benjamin grew up, after migrating from St. Croix. Charleston's Sephardic synagogue, Beth Elohim, became America's first Reform congregation, led by the fathers of Solomon Nuñes Carvalho and Judah P. Benjamin, among others.

The brilliant writer, critic and editor, Isaac Harby, was an important member of the Jewish community. He also founded an outstanding progressive school. Jews were in the vanguard of the city's trade and commerce. Theatre and opera thrived, as did all the arts. The names of those who were associated with Charleston's culture during these years were among America's finest artists: Thomas Sully, Raphael Peale, Samuel F. B. Morse, John James Audubon and Robert Miller, believed to be America's first native-born architect.

Solomon Nuñes Carvalho thrived in this environment. A descendant of Spanish and Portuguese Jews who traced their ancestry to the Portuguese Marquise de Pombal, his family, like others, had kin in the Caribbean islands of Barbados and Martinique. He benefited from a classical education, studying Latin and Greek. He enjoyed a privileged upbringing and maintained an aloof and aristocratic bearing throughout his life. Studying art early on, he was to dedicate much of his life to its pursuits. Age 19, he was already painting professionally.

Besides his devotion to art, Carvalho became a pioneer in American photography, an inventor, Jewish communal leader, writer and early explorer of the American West. He wrote of his adventures there and painted and photographed the grandeur of the Rocky Mountains, its Indians and settlers. Carvalho was an American Renaissance man who never forgot his Jewish heritage. In fact, he was active in religious affairs no matter where he lived throughout his life.

Carvalho was a traveler, too. In addition to Charleston, he lived in New York, Philadelphia, Baltimore, Los Angeles and Bridgetown, Barbados. Almost all these cities were to benefit from his presence.

In the early 1840s, the young painter added photography (then known as Daguerreotype) to his accomplishments. Samuel F. B. Morse, one of America's great artists and the inventor of the telegraph, instructed him in its application. Most of Carvalho's photographs and many of his canvasses have been lost. Yet it was through his talent in the application of these arts that he was to meet historic personages and embark upon the greatest adventure of his life.

In 1853, Carvalho was introduced to the famous explorer and fellow Charlestonian, John Charles Fremont. Known as "The Pathfinder," Fremont had already completed four well-publicized exploratory trips to the Far West. Even in 1853, however, much of the region still remained an unknown frontier, home to fur trappers, Indians and occasional settlers such as the Mormons, who were continuously moving West to avoid religious persecution.

Fremont's early attempts at photographing his travels were unsuccessful. He was resolved to return from his fifth and final exploration with good photographs. He wanted America and his prospective investors in the East to see what this unknown territory looked like.

On August 22, 1853, Carvalho accepted Fremont's invitation to accompany his fifth expedition across the Rockies. Although the photographic plates of this historic trip have been lost, Carvalho's descriptions of the scenic land remain in his book. His journey covered some of the highest and wildest parts of the United States. His book is filled with descriptions of adventure and adversity. The chronicle to this day remains an important record of the story of the exploration and settlement of the early West.

Carvalho was aware that he would be creating photographic images on glass plates (the photographic paper of the time,) using liquid developers in below-freezing - even sub-zero - weather. In addition to these problems, Fremont insisted on developed prints within an hour after being shot. Considering the state of photography in 1853 and the crude conditions Carvalho was working with in the field, it is a wonder he could produce any images. Still, he presented himself at St. Louis, the Gateway City to the West.

Called "Queen City of the Mississippi River," St. Louis was the jump-off point for the expedition. Departing by steamboat for Kansas, Fremont now advised Carvalho for the first time that the position of photographer was not yet his. Another Daguerrist by the name of Boman would compete with Carvalho in order that Fremont could assure himself of having the services of the best photographer available. Each man had his own system of photography, but Carvalho's incorporated some of his own improvements with respect to the application of the glass plate. This system impressed Fremont, who finally signed Carvalho on for the expedition.

There had been good reason for Fremont's concern. He and his father-in-law, the senator from Missouri Thomas Hart Benton, had personally funded earlier expeditions. Fremont was, in effect, a free-lancer, competing with government explorers. At stake was which set of explorers could convince America's railroad interests of the best route. For a new railroad system was being planned to carry a swiftly growing American people across the continent to the Pacific Ocean. Property along the selected route would be improved for commercial development, from the Great Divide to California.

Fremont insisted on producing photographs as proof that his route was the best one available. He planned to take Carvalho's photographic plates to the Eastern financiers and convince them their trains would be moving across the best trails possible, the ones he himself had pioneered. A quick photograph, processed on the spot and approved by Fremont, was what he needed - and insisted he get.

Another decision Fremont made, which was to cost great hardship as well as human life, was to embark upon a winter expedition. He intended to prove travel during the terrible Rocky Mountain winters was possible: up to that time, such an idea was considered unacceptable.

In his journals, Carvalho tells us that his fellow trekkers were not pleased with the bulky boxes in which he packed his equipment, saying they took up space for food and other necessaries during the cold winter. Members of the expedition often sabotaged his cargo and threw away vital equipment. The ever-vigilant Carvalho had to constantly secure his goods to the pack mules, picking up wayward material strewn along the trail.

Carvalho was not the only Jew on the expedition. Colonel Fremont's chief topographer, F. W. Egglofstein was also Jewish. Nor is it certain that they were the first of their religion to cross the Rocky Mountains. Historians cannot even say that Solomon Carvalho was the first Jew to photograph parts of the Rockies. He was, however, certainly the first to paint the grandeur of its forbidding mountains and its native Americans, photograph them, and then write extensively about the journey across the mountains.

The expedition was to last six months. The planned route took the explorers across Kansas, through lower Colorado, over the formidable Rockies at Cochetopa Pass, and through to the San Juan Mountains in southern Colorado. They would then pass into Utah and its maze of canyons and mesas, and cross Nevada into the Sierra Nevada Mountains. From there, the party would continue to the Pacific Ocean at San Francisco. It was an ambitious program, successfully executed although with much hardship.

They set out in September, when early fall weather delighted the travelers. Gold, red and russet leaves on the trees raised their spirits. But winter comes early to the Great Plains. Soon, ferocious winds and chest-high snows attacked them. Food became scarce. Clothing turned threadbare from constant wear and rubbing against trees and rocks aggravated the numbing cold. As time passed, feet began showing through tattered boots. The explorers moved through areas where there was no longer any color, only the blinding, swirling snows of the deep, white hell they had to plow through.

Carvalho's diary reports:

"The weather was excessively cold, the ice on the margin of either side of the river was over eighteen inches thick...It is most singular, that with all the exposure that I was subjected to on this journey, I never took the slightest cold, either in my head or in my chest; I do not recollect ever sneezing. While at home I ever was most susceptible to cold ... The thermometer indicated a great degree of cold; and (we) were standing almost to our middle in snow."

Physically frail, Carvalho suffered greatly. In keeping with his Grandee upbringing, he had packed Havana cigars, cognac and other luxuries that he now shared with his companions. These helped him to cope with knife-like winds, snow and biting cold. But not everyone was as fortunate. Oliver Fuller, one of Fremont's trail bosses who was physically robust and the strongest man in the camp, was the first to succumb to the elements. He died of exposure, proving that physical strength was not an automatic passport through the mountains.

Carvalho was enchanted with the wide spaces and natural beauty of the mountains. A product of the city, he had never seen anything close to these wide spaces filled with tall trees and deep valleys, with mighty rivers running below them. There, too, was the strange silence of the uninhabited woods and valleys. He photographed them, his camera high above the deep canyons.

More than once, he ignored Fremont's orders not to climb any higher to take pictures, as it was delaying the expedition. He climbed anyway, taking shots from the highest peaks he could scale, dragging his cumbersome equipment behind him.

During their travels, the explorers encountered bands of Indians. On one occasion, Carvalho cured the dyspepsia of a tribal chief after his shamans were unable to help him. In Carvalho's chest of luxury items, he carried Epsom salts and arrowroot, which he administered orally. The chief's stomach ailment miraculously disappeared.

The Indians considered Carvalho someone special. He enhanced his standing among the tribe when he applied chemicals from his kit to bracelets belonging to some of the Indian women. The metal gleamed and shone brightly, to the delight and wonder of the women. Aside from impressing Indians, Carvalho's "Pandora's box," as he called it, produced sperm candles at a critical moment when light was needed to take map bearings at night. "Fremont," Carvalho observed wryly, "gave little thought to where they were procured."

By February 1854, the cold became so deadly that Carvalho, Egglofstein and Fuller, who had fallen to the rear because of their duties, were forced to pull into the tiny Mormon settlement of Parowan. Carvalho was suffering from diarrhea and scurvy. He had also lost a great deal of weight: normally slight of build, he dropped 50 pounds and weighed less than 100 when he reached refuge. He tells us in his own words of the fearful condition in which he found himself:

"My hair was long, and had not known a comb for a month, my face was unwashed, and ground with the collected dirt of a similar period. Emaciated to a degree, my eyes sunken, and clothes all torn and tattered from haunting our animals through the bush. My hands were in a dreadful state; my fingers were frostbitten and split at every joint; and suffering at the same

time from diarrhoea,(sic) and symptoms of scurvy which broke out on me at Salt Lake City afterwards. I was in a situation truly to be pitied, and I do not wonder that the sympathies of the Mormons were excited in our favor, for my personal appearance being but a reflection of the whole party, we were indeed subjects for the exercise of the finer feelings of nature. When I entered Mr. Heap's house I saw three beautiful children. I covered my eyes and wept for joy to think I might yet be restored to embrace my own."

His companions, Fuller and Egglofstein, were also sick. The Mormons arranged to send both Carvalho and Egglofstein to Salt Lake City. The men were so sick and weak that they were unable to care for themselves. Unfortunately, Fuller had to be left behind. Among his other illnesses was a severe case of frostbite. When Fremont's scouts finally returned to rescue Fuller, he was near death and succumbed shortly thereafter.

Fremont realized that Carvalho and Egglofstein could no longer continue. Since they had substantially completed their work. Fremont went on without them.

At Salt Lake City, Carvalho began to mend. It was here that he met and was befriended by the legendary Mormon leader, Brigham Young. At the time, Young was engaged in a bitter struggle with hostile Indian tribes and the U.S. Government, which disapproved of the Mormon religious practice of polygamy. Carvalho had the rare privilege of observing the creation of a new state and the consolidation of a persecuted religion in unsettled Utah. As a Jew, he was not the object of conversion attempts, as Mormons believe Jews are a chosen people of God. Mormons closely identify themselves with the Hebrew Patriarchs. During his stay in Utah, Carvalho painted portraits of Brigham Young and several native Americans.

After 10 weeks at Salt Lake City, Carvalho continued on to Los Angeles. He set out by way of Provo, Utah, where he rendezvoused with Brigham Young. Young was at Provo to meet with the great Chief Walkara of the Ute tribe. He fought bloody battles with Mormon settlers and Young was determined to negotiate a peace or at least a standoff with the Utes. Young introduced Carvalho to the warrior chief and Carvalho's artistic studies of the Indians and his portrait of Walkara are well-known.

Continuing on to San Bernardino on June 9, Carvalho arrived in Los Angeles after a half-day's ride. During his stay in Los Angeles, he contacted the Jewish community. He helped organize the Los Angeles Hebrew Benevolent Society and was rewarded for his efforts by being elected an honorary member of the organization.

According to Carvalho's biographer, all the photographs and many of the paintings executed during this adventurous period of his life have been lost. Some historians speculate that they may be in an unopened packing crate in the Library of Congress. Is it possible that Fremont delivered them to the Library after showing them to his investors?

Carvalho returned to his home in Baltimore, where he remained for the rest of the decade. He was listed in the city's commercial directories as a Deguerrian, portrait painter and artist, maintaining a business establishment in the heart of Baltimore's downtown district.

Carvalho always maintained the Jewish side to his life. He learned much about his religion from his father and Uncle Manuel. David Nuñes Carvalho, Solomon's father, was an active member of Charleston's Beth Elohim. It was David, in concert with others, who was instrumental in making this synagogue America's first Reform congregation. David also acted as its Hazzan for a time. Manuel was Hazzan for synagogues in Barbados, Philadelphia, Charleston and New York, where he also taught religious school at Shearith Israel.

Despite his father's important role in the Reform movement, Carvalho retained a more traditional approach towards Judaism. When he moved to New York City, he became a member of Shearith Israel, and he continued his membership until his death.

In Baltimore, Carvalho entered into social life by becoming active in the Maryland Historical Society, the Maryland's Artist's association, and the Baltimore Chess Club. Characteristically, he also became involved in the city's religious life. In 1856, he helped found Beth Israel, a synagogue that followed the Spanish and Portuguese ritual and used English in the service. It was the first and last time a Sephardic synagogue was to exist in Baltimore. Financial difficulties caused the congregation to disband in 1859.

With his wife, the former Sarah Solis of Philadelphia (they were married by Isaac Leeser, a family friend,) he founded a religious school in which instruction was given in English and relied heavily upon female instructors. Sarah was a disciple of Rebecca Gratz, who was the foremost advocate of liberalizing religious instruction. The Baltimore Jewish community, heavily Germanic in its makeup, insisted in instructing its children in German. It would not accept female teachers. Despite the opposition from Baltimore's organized religious groups, the school went forward. It was the first of its kind in Baltimore and one of the first in the United States.

As much as his talents favored photography, art and communal organization, Carvalho had a difficult time making the kind of income he needed. Just prior to the Civil War, he turned his attention to physics. Other American painters, such as Morse, had abandoned fine arts to investigate science. In an age when the scientist was not necessarily university trained, men with talent and practical experience, impelled by natural curiosity, were making physical discoveries and inventing machines which made American life easier and more efficient.

Carvalho invented and obtained the patent for a more efficient boiler, which used energy created by its own steam. The Union Navy used it during the Civil War. In 1860, with war imminent, Carvalho left Baltimore for New York City.

The Union Navy's endorsement enhanced his new profession. He founded the Carvalho Steamworks, which was to provide his later years with financial security. He and his beloved wife Sarah ran a religious school for children with less opposition than they encountered in Baltimore. As his father had done, he too wrote religious tracts, which were never published.

Living in the sylvan recesses of the Bronx, on what is now Tremont Avenue, Carvalho was forced to abandon painting because of failing eyesight. He died in 1897, and was buried at the cemetery of the Spanish and Portuguese synagogue in New York City.

Solomon Nuñes Carvalho's pioneering experiences were memorialized in his book, *"Incidents of Travel and Adventure in the Far West with Col. Freemont's Last Expedition Across the Rocky Mountains."* The book was published in 1860. Carvalho unwisely sold all rights to his manuscript for a few hundred dollars. Had he held out for royalties, he would have reaped financial success from his efforts, for the book sold well. Carvalho became a celebrity. Had Fremont received the Republican nomination for the Presidency, Carvalho might have been Collector of Customs for Baltimore. Abraham Lincoln's selection by the party dashed those plans.

Unlike the lost photographs, some of Carvalho's paintings are in museums and private collections. His painting, "Child with a Rabbit," appeared on bank notes in countries throughout the Western Hemisphere, making it one of the most widely circulated works of art in its time. Aside from Brigham Young and Walkara, he painted portraits of Lincoln, Touro and Isaac Leeser.

What makes Solomon Nuñes Carvalho's life significant is that he was always an American and always a Jew. When he traveled through the frozen hell of the mountains he never forgot his religion. Wherever he lived, he balanced the two sides of his life. He did not deny his religion to be an American and he did not sublimate his Americanism to practice his religion.

In his chronicles, Carvalho tells us that during the most dire moments of the expedition, when the cold was unbelievably bitter and food ran out, Fremont, who had seen cannibalism on one of his previous expeditions, forced his men at gunpoint to swear not to repeat such savagery. The men were prepared to slaughter their mules for food. Despite his desperate hunger, Carvalho hesitated to eat meat that was not kosher. He resolved the problem by reminding himself that it was his duty as a Jew to remain alive. In the frozen regions of the Far West, Carvalho faced his religious obligations and resolved them according to his faith.

During these desperate times, Carvalho remembered the words of the Psalmist. He wrote that he *"felt perfectly assured of my final deliverance,"* and he quoted Hebrew scripture:

"They wandered in the wilderness in a solitary way: They found no city to dwell in.

"Hungry and thirsty their souls fainted within them. Then they cried unto the Lord in their trouble, and he delivered them out of their distresses.

" And he led them forth by the right way and they might go to a city of habitation.

"Oh that men would praise the Lord for his goodness, and for his wonderful works to the children of men."

Solomon Nunes Carvalho, self portrait, Library of Congress
LC-USZ62-61105

Indian Village by Solomon Nunes Carvalho, Library of Congress, LC-USZ62-9065

"Abraham Lincoln and Diogenes" 1865, by Solomon Nunes
Carvalho, Rose Museum, Brandeis University, Waltham, Mass.
Gift of Justin Turner, Los Angeles.

MORDECAI MANUEL NOAH

*"Where can we plead the cause of independence for the
Children of Israel with greater confidence than in the
cradle of American liberty?"*

Mordecai Manuel Noah

For three decades before the Civil War, Mordecai Manuel
Noah was America's most well known Jew, according to commentators of the day. Born in Philadelphia in 1785, he was a
descendant of Portuguese Jews who came to the United States
before the Revolutionary War. His great-grandmother, Zipporah
Nuñez Machado, escaped the Portuguese Inquisition, shed her
forced Catholicism, then affirmed her Jewishnesss by marrying
the Reverend Machado, Hazzan of New York's Spanish and
Portuguese Synagogue. His father, Manuel Mordecai Noah,
fought with the Continental Army. Noah's maternal grandfather, Jonas Phillips, was also a Revolutionary War patriot.

Mordecai Manuel Noah and Uriah Phillips Levy, America's
first Jewish naval officer, were cousins. They shared the same
grandfather (Jonas Phillips) and the same great-grandmother
(Zipporah Machado). Grandfather Phillips took on the respon-

sibility of raising Noah when he was orphaned as a young boy of four. He was a precocious child who, although apprenticed to do craftwork, soon demonstrated a talent for writing, organization and ultimately, politics. During his lifetime, he was to achieve success in many careers: editor, playwright, diplomat, politician, judge, sheriff and spokesman for Jewish communal affairs.

Despite all his accomplishments, Noah is not well known to contemporary American Jews. But he does have an important place in American Jewish history. He was the first in the United States to publicly concern himself with a homeland for his co-religionists.

At first, Noah conceived of a Zion within the borders of the United States. But a decade before his death in 1851, he was to publicly and seriously call upon Jews to settle in Palestine and create a homeland through their own political efforts and the work of their hands. Noah was to precede Theodore Herzl's vision of Zion by half a century.

Before Noah was busying himself with this prophetic activity, he lived a fascinating and exciting life; one which deserves attention. His career began in 1809. As editor of "The City Gazette" in Charleston, South Carolina, Noah used the newspaper as his personal political sounding board. He regularly attacked Great Britain, against which he urged America to go to war.

At the time, Charleston was a prosperous seaport engaged in significant trade with England. The citizenry had no wish for war and Noah often battled with the townspeople over his political views. They were deadly serious arguments, one quarrel ending in a duel in which he killed his opponent.

It was in Charleston that Noah first tried his hand at play writing. His initial effort, "Paul and Alexis," or "Orphans of the Rhine," met with great success. It was performed in Charleston, and then traveled to England. When it returned to America it was successfully staged at the Park Theatre in New York City.

In 1812, Noah embarked upon his public career. He was appointed American Counsul to Tunis, with a special mission: obtain the release through ransom of imprisoned American sailors held by Algerians. Allotted a specific sum with which to accomplish this task, Noah spent more. He had to dip into his own pocket to complete his mission.

His instructions were explicit:

"You may probably devise means for the liberation of our unfortunate countrymen at Algiers (the captured American seamen) ... should you find a suitable channel through which you can negotiate their immediate release, you are authorised to go as far as $3,000 a man, but a less sum may probably effect the object.. Whatever may be the result of the attempt, you will, for obvious reasons, not let it be understood to proceed from this government, but rather from the friends of the parties themselves."

On his way to North Africa, Noah was captured by the British. The naval War of 1812 had begun and he was shipped to England where although a prisoner, he was allowed to remain free on parole, because of his diplomatic status. At the same time, his cousin Uriah Phillips Levy languished in Britain's Dartmoor prison as a captive of war.

There were 11 crewmembers of the brig, *"Edwin"* out of Salem, Massachusetts being held by Algerian pirates. Noah was to draw the necessary sums from the State Department and swiftly dispatch the seamen to the United States after their release. He believed he had authority, but apparently others had different ideas about his mission.

Political enemies in the United States used this mission to Noah's disadvantage and agitated for his recall. They claimed he had gone beyond his specific orders. The whole affair turned nasty when Secretary of State James Monroe wrote to Noah, dismissing him. Monroe said his Consul's religion was an obstacle to the successful accomplishment of his task. Some writers have claimed that by advancing the theory that America was not a Christian country, Noah invited official disapproval. But eventually, he was vindicated. His overpayments were approved and he was reimbursed for monies advanced.

Historian Jonathan Sarna, in his biography of Noah, "Jacksonian Jew: The Two Worlds of Mordecai Manuel Noah," suggests that Noah brought the woes upon himself by keeping less than adequate financial records. He further states that the tale of the duel resulting in death was probably a myth.

A footnote to Noah's tenure in Tunis should be of interest to international lawyers. While Noah was stationed in Tunis, America was at war with England. A Yankee privateer pulled into port with three captured vessels, carrying valuable cargo. As Consul, Noah arranged for the prizes to be sold at auction pursuant to the rules of war. The English Minister argued that because of Tunis' treaty with England, no Christian country could sell captured British vessels or prize cargo in her ports.

"Not so," Noah argued. "The United States of America is not a Christian country." He produced copies of the Constitution to prove his point. It revealed that America was non-sectarian, and he cited some treaties and other precedent showing his country's position on that point. The Bey of Tunis agreed and permitted the sale. Some historians believe this incident may be what Monroe was alluding to when he said that Noah's religion was an obstacle to his consular duties.

Noah wrote an apology. He related how he dispensed charity to Christians in Tunisia, and permitted Catholics and Protestants access to the American Counsul.

"The poor Christian slaves when they wanted a favour, came to me. The Jews alone asked nothing from me. Why then am I to be persecuted for my religion?" Noah asked.

In 1818, President Madison wrote an amiable letter to

Noah, affirming that the government of the United States sought freedom for every religious sect. He expressed pleasure that the matter of Noah's accounts had been successfully settled. Some historians maintain that President Madison was unaware of Noah's dilemma. The theory is that Secretary of State Monroe may have been a tool of Noah's enemies.

His diplomatic career behind him, Noah left for New York in 1816. He would embark upon the two careers for which he would become well known: politics and writing. He became editor of a succession of New York City newspapers, "The National Advocate," the "New York Enquirer," the "Evening Star," the "Commercial Advertiser," "The Union," and "The Times and Messenger."

In 1819, after he was absolved of all charges concerning his role as Consul in Tunisia, he wrote, "Travels in England, France, Spain and the Barbary States." Noah detailed his observations of Europe, his captivity in England, and his work in releasing the American seamen from slavery. He was becoming well known as editor and author.

He returned to playwriting. Never a great dramatist, he was nevertheless an accomplished and successful writer. Noah's career as a dramatist deserves some mention and examination. Until he began writing for the theatre, American playwrights did not concern themselves with America. Noah should be recognized as the first to incorporate themes of patriotism, love of country, and American historical events into his plays.

Historian Lee M. Friedman, in his 1948 book, "Pilgrims in a New Land," devotes a complete chapter to Noah's career as playwright. Mentioned prominently in that chapter is the play, "She Would Be a Soldier." Written in 1820, it is the tale of a woman who disguised herself as a male, to be a soldier during the Revolutionary War in order to be near her lover. The play contains much patriotism: it is the first time such themes were brought to the public in any American theatre.

The play must have had some merit. It was well received

and was shown at theatres in the United States until 1848. It was reprinted in 1918 in "Representative Plays by American Dramatists." More than 100 years after it's initial publication, the play was analyzed in "Annals of the New York Stage 1927." It was deemed a significant play of its time.

Noah was always conscious of the effect he wished to have on his audience. In 1819, he wrote,

"An American audience, I have no doubt, would be pleased with an American play, if the performance afforded as much gratification as a good English one; but they pay their money to be pleased, and if we cannot afford pleasure, we have no proscriptive right to ask for approbation."

In all, Noah wrote 11 plays. Many had patriotic themes. One, the "Grecian Captive," told the story of the Greek struggle for independence. Friedman tells us that the play was actually written for Noah's uncle, the actor Aaron Phillips. While none of his plays is remembered today, Noah did reflect his love and pride for America through this medium. He exhibited the same feelings that his cousin Uriah Levy showed for his country. Is it any wonder? Both were fourth-generation Americans, infused with their patriotism by their grandfather, Jonas Phillips.

Noah was the most active Jew in northern politics during the years preceding the Civil War. He entered with a passion and a flourish fired by his egoism. He held the office of High Sheriff of New York in 1822, and was then appointed Surveyor of the Port of New York by President Andrew Jackson. Noah was Sachem of Tammany Hall, the political organization that controlled the Democratic party in New York and still does to this day.

In 1841, Noah was appointed a judge. His old journalistic rival, James Gordon Bennett, attacked him. Controversy surrounded his tenure at this post, until he resigned rather than preside over the trial of a congressman who was a boyhood friend. The congressman was being tried for forgery. Bennett's reward for his attacks on a judge was a monetary fine. Like his cousin, Uriah Levy, Noah often would feel the sting of anti-Semitism. When he received his judicial appointment, an opponent quipped, "Who is this Jew that he should be allowed to hang a Christian?" Noah retorted, "Pretty sort of Christian, that he should require hanging at anyone's hands."

Together with his strong love for America, Noah also fostered a loyalty to his Jewish roots. He was one of the few Jews in the North who held public office and was always before the public because of his plays and journalism. He was constantly under attack and reminded of his heritage. Unflattering political cartoons appeared showing him with the exaggerated hooked nose associated with the Jew.

For all his successes in his own time, Noah is better remembered today as a genuine, homegrown American Zionist. He first felt the United States could be a homeland for Jews and later dreamed of a Jewish state in Palestine. This was decades before Theodore Herzl's Zion would be set before the world. In 1825, he realized the dream he had been nurturing for almost a decade. At a synagogue dedication in 1818, he made remarks alluding to a Jewish homeland, which he had been thinking about for some time. He proposed to create a place where Jews could go and live unmolested; where they could be farmers or traders, teachers or professionals in a place where they could rule themselves and control their own lives.

He acquired a 17,000 acre tract of land at Grand Island near Buffalo, on the Niagra River. Noah called the place Ararat, "A City of Refuge for the Jews," and he invited world Jewry to settle there. What occurred later reduced his accomplishments to historians, most tending to relegate him to a minor role. Some even treat Noah as if he were a buffoon. This is unfair, as Noah had a real interest in bettering the position of the world's Jews. Things did not go smoothly at the inauguration of Ararat, on

September 15, 1825. Not enough watercraft was available to ferry people over to the island for the ceremony. Noah chose the Episcopal Church in Buffalo as the alternate site for his Jewish-oriented ceremonies. Resplendent in a crimson silk robe with ermine trimmings, he led a procession through the streets of Buffalo, accompanied by a marching band, military units, government dignitaries and fraternal orders, each in their unique bright attire. For this, he received sharp criticism from Jewish leaders.

Noah created the title of "Governor and Judge of Israel" for himself. The ceremonies included his long presentation, topped off by a thunderous 24-gun salute as a finale.

At a distance of almost 200 years, we can appreciate Noah's understanding and manipulation of the dramatic, but we can also understand why commentators downplayed him. Ararat was a flop. Its acreage lay uncultivated, its promises of a Jewish autonomous state unfulfilled. The cornerstone, which was never set in place, is now one of the great attractions at the Buffalo and Erie County Historical Society. It travels throughout America on loan.

Historian Jonathan Sarna believes that Noah's Zionist efforts resulted from his discouraging realization that despite the many generations of Jewish experience in America, they had only a fragile hold in its society.

Noah did not abandon his dream. Twenty years later, he was to address the public in two serious discourses that were later published as a book. On October 28 and then December 2, 1844, he argued for support - not only from Jews but of Christians as well - for the establishment of a Jewish state in what was then known as Palestine.

He was eloquent and prophetic in his pleas for support from all corners of American society:

" ... *Where can we plead the cause of independence for the Children of Israel with greater confidence than in the cradle of*

American liberty?" he argued. "Where ask for toleration and kindness for the seed of Abraham, if we not find it among the descendants of the Pilgrims?"

"... This, my countrymen, will be your judgement - your opinion - when asked to cooperate in giving freedom to the Jews ...

" ... the first step is to solicit from the Sultan of Turkey permission for the Jews to purchase and hold land; to build houses .. in perfect security ...

" ... the whole territory surrounding Jerusalem including the villages, Hebron, Safat, Tyre, also Beyroot, Jaffa and other ports of the Mediterranean will be occupied by enterprising Jews. The valleys of the Jordan will be filled with agriculturists from the north of Germany, Poland and Russia..."

Aside from his work in Zionism, Noah was involved in the daily affairs of New York's Jewish community. He served as the head of the Hebrew Benevolent Society and the Jewish Charity Organization. He also published a translation of the "Book of Jashar." When he died in 1851, Mordecai Manuel Noah was the last Jew to be buried within the municipal confines of New York City.

Noah deserves to be recognized as an important member of America's pre-Civil War Jewish community. He was visible to Jews and Christians and was one of the first of his religion to be appointed to a diplomatic post. While Noah's experience was not a happy one, he showed grit and determination. He would not be bullied because he was a Jew. He persisted until he cleared his name and reputation. He engaged in the political life of his community, holding positions of both national and state importance. His presence at such an early stage of a new country was an example to others of his faith who learned that their religion would not be an insurmountable handicap.

As a writer, Noah held important positions as editor of several newspapers. He was free to express political and social ideas, something most Jews throughout the world could not do at the time. He felt comfortable enough with his position as editor and his religion, to argue about Sunday closing laws. In 1848, in editorials of the "Sunday Times," and "Noah's Weekly Messenger," he sided with a ban on Sunday commerce. It may not have been a popular position as far as his fellow Jews were concerned, but he set forth his position clearly, even explaining it did not violate the rights of the "Hebrew."

Noah's opinion on this subject was of great interest to the Jewish public at large, since he was a prominent co-religionist.

Isaac Leeser opposed this view and published articles against Noah's stand. This illustrates that before the Civil War America's Jews were free to express themselves even about the government's laws and, more importantly, that Jews were not monolithic in their approach to their government and its legislation.

Finally, Noah turned out to be a visionary through his experiment with American Zionism and his later discourses on Jewish settlement in Palestine.

Noah can be summed up in his own words as put down in one of his editorials:

"Respect to the law of the land we live in, is the first duty of good citizens of all denominations."

The Ararat Stone, Buffalo & Erie County Historical Society, Buffalo, New York

REBECCA GRATZ

Most American children attending Jewish religious schools today receive instruction in English. Their teachers are both men and women. In addition to Torah and Talmud, they learn other subjects in classes shared by boys and girls. It wasn't always so.

In the 19th century, as America's Jewish population was increasing, synagogues established religious schools to attend to their community's needs. German and Polish institutions taught in German or Yiddish. Sephardim taught in Spanish or Portuguese. Almost all the schools forbade female teachers and very few permitted girls as pupils.

It was obvious to one young woman, daughter of a wealthy Philadelphia family, that Jewish religious education needed to be tailored to the special needs of American children. Her name was Rebecca Gratz and she was to influence American Jewry for much of the 19th century.

Gratz holds a special place in American history as a philanthropist, educator, commentator on her times, a letter-writer, friend of prominent Americans and, perhaps, the model for the Jewish heroine of Sir Walter Scott's "Ivanhoe." Although she was associated with the American Jewish community, she moved easily across many levels of both Jewish and Christian society because of her family's privileged circumstances.

Born in 1771, Rebecca Gratz lived her entire life in Philadelphia. Before the Revolutionary War, the Gratz family was one of the wealthiest in the thirteen colonies. They had trading connections throughout North America. Their wealth and sophistication gave them entré into Philadelphia's high society. Rebecca received a fine education, which held her in good stead. Never concerned with financial security and unmarried, she devoted much of her life to public concerns. During her lifetime, she was America's most well known Jewess.

As Rebecca Gratz was growing up, a religious education was not available for all Jewish male children. Girls, for the most part, could expect no formal religious training whatsoever. The first Jewish school established in America began in 1728, while America was still an English colony. The school was founded by New York's Sephardic synagogue, Shearith Israel. In 1755, secular and religious education was joined in this school. It was innovative for the times.

In 1802, the school was reorganized, taking the name "Polonies Talmud Torah," after its benefactor, Abraham Polonies. It, and others like it throughout the United States, required attendance during weekdays. In 1854, the school and its sponsoring organization, Shearith Israel, received the total sum of $13,000 through a bequest in Judah Touro's will. The Polonies school still exists.

Rebecca Gratz forever changed the way Jewish children received religious instruction in the United States. She observed that in Philadelphia, Protestant religious schools were in session just one day a week. Convinced that the same should hold true for Jewish education, in 1833 she prepared and organized the prototype of the Jewish Sunday school as it still exists today in the United States. She called it "The Hebrew Day School Society." Gratz headed this organization as supervisor and President for 26 years. The program inaugurated English instruction and also qualified women as teachers.

Gratz felt that one-day a week for education was better than no education at all for young Jewish children. Many Jews opposed this idea, as emulating Christians.

At first, her ideas met with much opposition. In Baltimore, one of Gratz' disciples was Sarah Solis and her husband Solomon Nuñes Carvalho. They introduced the English-speaking Sunday school over violent objections from the city's rabbis. Most rabbis in new immigrant communities insisted on conducting religious services and offering sermons in German or Yiddish. The Carvalhos also attempted to establish a religious school that would serve the whole community instead of each congregation establishing its own. That was also an advanced idea: their efforts met with mixed success.

Rebecca Gratz' life was also devoted to helping others. She was only 20 when she became secretary of the first institution in Philadelphia to assist poor women and children. She founded it, with her mother and a score of other women, as a non-sectarian organization.

In 1815, touched by the difficult conditions Jewish immigrants were encountering, she organized the Female Hebrew Benevolent Society. It was the first Jewish philanthropic society in the United States, and was the model for others to follow. She then began the first Orphan Society for Jews in America, acting as its secretary for four decades, from 1819 to 1859.

Determined not to marry outside her religion, Gratz remained single, although she is said to have loved John Ewing, son of a well-known Protestant clergyman and educator.

Her letters clearly show her strong opposition to intermarriage. In one, written in 1817 to her friend, Mrs. Matilda Hoffman of New York City, she states:

"I believe it is impossible to reconcile a matrimonial engagement between persons of so different a creed (Jew and non-Jew) without requiring one or the other to yield ... where a family of children are to be brought up, it appears necessary that parents should agree on so important a subject."

Rebecca Gratz was also concerned with the welfare of European Jews who were undergoing turmoil and upheaval. Writing again to her friend in New York City, she said:

"The late persecutions of the Jews in Europe has greatly interested me in their fate - I wonder they do not come to America, if they could only bring enough with them, to feed and cloth (sic) themselves I should think that they would be happier under such a government, than with the precarious wealth they accumulate under their oppressors ... "

Gratz lived with brothers, nephews, cousins and in-laws, all of who were as concerned as she was with the plight of Jews being persecuted overseas. In one petition addressed to the U.S. Senate in 1854, concerning the equal treatment of American Jews in foreign countries, all of its six signatories were of the immediate Gratz family.

Aside from her deep concern for Jews, orphans and the destitute, Rebecca could be chatty, if somewhat formal, in her letters. They are filled with personal information about mutual friends and family in places like New York, Savannah, Charleston and abroad. The American Jewish Historical Society has thousands of pages of her correspondence. The collection does not represent the totality of her letter writing.

Because of her comfortable financial circumstances, Rebecca Gratz was able to have several of her portraits painted by some of America's finest contemporary artists. Today, we have the opportunity to see her as talented artists such as Thomas Sully saw her. Sully painted several portraits, one of which only recently has proven to be of someone other than Gratz. His authenticated portrait of her, however, portrays her as a beautiful young girl.

Matilda Hoffman introduced her special friend, Washington Irving, to Rebecca. He was one of early America's noted authors. Often entertained by the Gratz family, his relationship to Rebecca resulted in a legend that may or may not be based in fact.

When Matilda died, Irving was heartbroken. He left for Europe. There, he struck up a strong friendship with Sir Walter Scott. Scott was in the process of outlining his next novel, "Ivanhoe." During conversations, the two writers discussed the book's characters. Irving is supposed to have drawn glowing descriptions of Rebecca Gratz. Scott, it is said, was determined to put this Jewish heroine into his tale of knights, chivalry, and their contacts with the medieval English Jewish community in the city of York.

After reading "Ivanhoe" in 1820, Rebecca Gratz wrote to a relative, asking her if she had read the novel and requesting her opinion *"of my namesake, Rebecca."* Was she aware that she was perhaps the model for Scott's heroine?

This great lady lived for 88 years. Much of her work was not only visionary, but also enduring. Her efforts revolutionized general Jewish education in America. Her association with charitable organizations, religious and secular, is in the strong tradition of Jewish tzedakah and mitzvah.

In her "Recollections of the First Hebrew Sunday School," Gratz' grandniece Rosa Mordecai writes of her famous grandaunt presiding over the school at Zane Street. Dressed in *"plain black,"* she recalled, *"with white collar and cuffs, close fitting bonnet over her curled front, which time never touched with grey; giving her, even in her most advanced years, a youthful appearance."*

Starting each school session with prayer, Gratz gained the support of two of America's most influential religious leaders of the time, Isaac Leeser and Sabato Morais. Both were regular visitors to the school, answering questions of both pupils and teachers.

Judah Touro, the American philanthropist, recognized her work by leaving three bequests to organizations closely associated with her: The Female Hebrew Benevolent Society, The Hebrew Education Society of Philadelphia, and the United Hebrew Benevolent Society of Philadelphia. The bequests left by Touro to these organizations totaled $26,000, a substantial sum for the times.

History is filled with people who struggle against their circumstances to rise above them. Rebecca Gratz was born into privileged circumstances, yet she is an example of the classic Jewish concept of Tzedakah as justice. A woman who could have very easily spent her days at ease, she chose instead to work among the poor and destitute, helping them to lift themselves from the depths of poverty. She understood that education, always a Jewish concern, should be made available to every Jewish child. As a visionary, she went further. She insisted that instruction should be in English, the language that young American children were using to the exclusion of European tongues their parents brought with them to America.

Gratz broke sexual barriers. Not only would young girls attend religious school, but qualified adult women would teach them. Her ideas and visions were so successful they still work today.

This woman who traveled with the upper classes, who saw Jews marrying out of their religion yet who remained steadfast to her principle of refusing to intermarry, could show compassion to those caught in the web of such relationships. An aunt married a New York Schuyler over the vehement objections of her father, who then refused to have further contact with her. On his deathbed, through Rebecca's efforts, he forgave his daughter. It must have been an emotional reunion: a dying father, 92 years old, and his tearful daughter, finally reconciled. It is incidents such as this and others about which she wrote in her many letters concerning difficult intermarriages that may have left her wary.

Gratz personified noblesse oblige. For all her good work, she may have been a somewhat imposing figure, for she is described in later life as stuffy and Victorian, even prissy.

When Gratz died, she was deeply mourned, not only by Jews but also by others who recognized her unique contribution to American life. She is buried in the historic graveyard of Philadelphia's Mikveh Israel synagogue, now part of Independence National Historical Park. The cemetery was originally purchased by the Levy family in 1738 from William Penn. In 1766, it was expanded to permit the burial of Philadelphia's Jews. In addition to many other distinguished Jews buried here, you will find the grave of Haym Salomon.

Thomas Sully portrait of Rebecca Gratz, Delaware Historical Society

Rebecca Gratz in her later years; American Jewish Historical Society

JUDAH TOURO

"...he saw that the work was at length accomplished, and that his pious intentions, which he had so long indulged had at last been carried into effect ..."

Reverend Isaac Lesser

Paintings and photographs portraying Judah Touro are no indication of his largess. Here is a dour man, dressed in somber, conservative clothing. His head is topped with a black stovepipe hat. His mouth looks as if it had never known a smile. Yet this man's generosity is an American legend, not only after his death, but during his lifetime as well. He is an example of how Jews approach civic responsibility. His example impelled not just Jews, but all Americans with resources to help the needy.

He is pictured as being a modest man. His employees said that he was kind, generous and loyal. This extremely successful businessman was known among his colleagues to be fair and honest. He is also described as closemouthed and strange.

During his lifetime, Judah Touro responded to such diverse causes as poorhouses in his hometown of New Orleans, a hospice in Jerusalem, and the assistance of fellow Jews isolated in the vast Chinese interior. Most of his philanthropy was directed to non-Jewish institutions, since he abandoned the practice of Judaism early in his life. He may well have been America's first public philanthropist, and a century and a half after his death his name lives on for his generous works, as do many of the institutions he endowed so long ago.

This native New Englander turned successful Southern entrepreneur was born on the eve of the Revolutionary War. He was the son of the Sephardic hazzan of Newport's Jewish community. One hundred fifty years after his death, his name and memory still grace three synagogues, a hospital, a college, a park, and many streets throughout the United States.

In an era when public philanthropy was practically unknown, and charity was limited to assistance within family circles, Touro was one of the first Americans to bestow significant sums upon worthy public causes. In 1854, when the dollar had a considerably greater value than it does today, Touro left the huge sum of $387,000 to needy Jewish and Christian institutions all over the United States. He endowed almost every known synagogue in America and some of the religious schools, too. Many of them continue operating to this day.

Public charity, even among individual Jews, was not widely practiced in America before Touro. In his book, "Wills of Early New York Jews," Prof. Leo Hershkowitz of Queens College compiled wills of the period 1704-1799. Very few Jews gave to charitable organizations. Those who did left money to Shearith Israel, New York's only synagogue at the time. There was a dearth of charities, as we understand them today.

Jews routinely use the Hebrew word, Tzedakah, to describe acts of charity. The correct translation, however, is "justice," because for a Jew to render assistance to others is not understood as an act of charity, but rather as dispensation of justice to the needy.

Perhaps another word that explains the concept is "fairness." In Judaism it is just, right, and fair that one favored by God with a bounty of material riches, share them with those not so fortunate.

Jewish religious ethics also require that the dignity of the recipient of Tzedakah be maintained. The great medieval Jewish philosopher and thinker Moses Ben Maimon, known to the world as Maimonides, designated eight levels of charity.

The first level, basic giving, is to assist only when requested to do so by the needy. The highest order of assistance - the eighth level - is to help someone to earn a living with dignity. This is accomplished by placing him in a position of self-help and avoids the necessity for his seeking charity in the future.

This illuminating principle was translated at the end of the 19th century into Jewish Loan Societies. They were established to help new immigrants to America. The loans were interest free. The idea of the Loan Society and its interest-free loans comes from Exodus 22:24, which says: "If thou loan money to my people, to the poor by thee, thou shalt not lay upon him interest."

The Jews of Central and Eastern Europe who landed on these shores beginning in the 1880s were not the first to benefit from Jewish self-help. This tradition among American Jews goes back to the very first who arrived in New Amsterdam in 1654.

Fleeing from Portuguese persecution in Brazil, this band of 23 Jews was captured by pirates. By the time they were rescued they had been stripped of their possessions, lost their children through kidnapping, survived beatings, and other indignities. They arrived in New Amsterdam not only penniless, but in debt for their passage to the French captain who rescued them. Captain De La Motte had a claim he pursued in the Dutch Colonial court. To add to these woes, the Colonial governor, Peter Stuyvesant, wanted no Jews in his colony. Certainly, they could not stay if they were to become charity cases.

The situation was resolved when the Jewish community,

both in Holland and New Amsterdam (some of the 23 wrote home and received funds to tide them over,) guaranteed that no Jews would become a public charge. The idea of Jews becoming public charges has been something American Jews have since avoided in communities throughout America.

It is true that a few decades before Touro's will, American Jews had founded some hospitals and other charitable institutions. They were not the efforts of individuals, but of the community as a group. Prior to the beginning of the 20th century, Jewish charity and help were the works of the synagogues. And there were few synagogues in America during the middle of the 19th century.

Judah Touro filled the role of the personal donor close to Maimonides's eighth level. Much of his giving, both before and after his life, fits the category of one who gives without being asked, with the blessing that the gift will help the donee toward self-sufficiency.

Touro's life was one of contradictions. This wealthy merchant grew up in poverty, one of three children of Isaac de Abraham Touro, hazzan of Congregation Yeshuat Israel in Newport, Rhode Island. It was the second oldest Jewish congregation in America, founded four years after Shearith Israel in New York.

Isaac Touro was a native of Holland who migrated to the colonies. Around 1758 he secured the appointment as hazzan to Newport's congregation. It was he who performed the ceremony of consecration when the now-famous synagogue building was completed in 1763.

When the Revolutionary War broke out, Isaac Touro chose not to take the oath of loyalty to the rebel colonies. He sided with the English. After the British Army entered Newport, most of the Jewish community fled to Massachusetts and Philadelphia. But the Touros finally wound up in the British colony of Jamaica when Isaac petitioned General Sir Guy

Carleton for help in emigrating. Isaac died in 1784, while acting as hazzan for the Jamaican community of Kingston.

With no money and faced with supporting two sons and a daughter, Isaac's widow Reyna Touro returned to Boston to live with her brother Moses Michael Hayes. Hayes raised the Touro children as his own when Reyna died.

The three Touros could not have had a better role model for their upbringing. Hayes was Boston's most prominent and respected Jewish citizen. He was involved in shipping, insurance, and banking. Despite being so active, he still lived the life of an observant Jew. Boston had no synagogues at the time. The Hayes home was used for religious services. It contained a library with many religious books. Moses Hayes taught the Touro boys the Jewish way of life, including charity: he was a founder of one of America's great hospitals, Massachusetts General.

Moses Hayes put Judah Touro and his brother Abraham to work. The training was to be invaluable to them both. For Judah, it included a trip abroad in 1798 as a representative of the cargo. Attacked by a French privateer, he fought alongside the rest of the crew and was able to help preserve the profits of the voyage.

Judah left for New Orleans in 1801, when it was a French territory with a population of 800. Two years later, through the Louisiana Purchase, the United States bought all of France's property south of Canada. Touro is generally believed to have been the first Jewish settler in this American colony. New Orleans became a boomtown. With his acquired knowledge of international trade, Touro became a wealthy man. He was involved in all manner of trade, including shipping.

It has been said that Touro left Boston after he fell in love with his cousin, one of Hayes' daughters. Hayes would not permit them to marry because they were first cousins. The tale has never been proven. But it is a fact that Touro remained a bachelor all his life. His brother Abraham and their sister remained in New England. Abraham also prospered and dispensed charity according to the lessons learned from his uncle.

During the War of 1812, 39-year old Touro volunteered to defend New Orleans. A militia was marshaled under Andrew Jackson to defend the city. Touro was badly wounded during the battle and left on the battlefield with a massive wound in his leg. He might have died, but was discovered by his lifelong friend, Shepard Rezin, who nursed him back to health.

Touro was not at this time a regular member of the New Orleans Jewish community. In fact, he had remained outside of his religion for a long time. His charities and good works were dispensed largely within Christian and laic institutions. New Orleans' steamy tropical climate was host to regular outbreaks of yellow fever. Not only did he fund the medical battles fought against the pestilence, he founded the now-famous Touro Clinic, one of the South's great medical institutions

It was his friendships with Gershom Kursheedt, a founder and President of New Orleans' first synagogue, and the outstanding religious leader Issac Leeser, that changed him. Kursheedt directed Touro toward charitable works within New Orleans' Jewish community. He was to become one of the executors of Touro's will. Leeser convinced Touro to become more active in the Jewish community at large and to grant financial aid to Jewish organizations throughout America.

Touro became one of the founders of synagogue Nefuzoth Yehudah in New Orleans, which followed the same Sephardic ritual ministered by his father in Newport. In 1850, four years before his death, he was again becoming active in the faith of his fathers. Touro purchased an Episcopalian church for the use of his new congregation. With both Leeser and Kursheedt beside him, the 75-year-old benefactor laid the cornerstone for the reconstructed synagogue. That congregation is today known as the Touro Synagogue of New Orleans.

Here is Isaac Leeser's description of that important day in the life of New Orleans' Jews:

"Mr. T himself was greatly moved. It was a glorious day in his bright life, a bright hour too on which he might reflect with pleasure and gratification to the latest moment of his earthly existence. Many there are who are blessed with wealth and ample possessions, but few who have the heart to dispose of it in their lifetime; they clutch their gold as the dearest thing on earth and cannot think of distributing it till after death has closed their career. But here was a man who had toiled as hard as any of them, who knew as well as any the value of gold and lands; and yet he could part with a large portion freely and cheerfully."

Touro himself laid the cornerstone for the new synagogue. In keeping with his characteristic modesty, only 10 people were present for the ceremony. The stone had the following legend:

"This building was at first erected and used as a place of worship for non-Israelites, but through the liberality of Judah Touro (a son of Israel), it was purchased and donated to the Portuguese Hebrew Congregation of the Dispersed of Judah, as a place of prayer to the most high God, the sole Lord and Creator, to whom be praised everlastingly. In testimony of which this stone is solemnly deposited beneath the portals through which the faithful are to enter to praise the Lord."

New Orleans, 3d Sivan, 14th May, 5610 (1850), the seventy-fourth year of the Independence of America.

When his brother Abraham died in 1822, he, too, left money to several public institutions, including Massachusetts General Hospital in Boston and the synagogue in Newport where their father had served as Hazzan. It had not yet assumed the name of Touro synagogue. He also willed Judah the sum of $100,000. Instead of keeping the money, Touro let it draw interest and used it for charity.

Judah Touro died in 1854. His will, which was made public that same year, must have created a sensation. Over 53 institutions were given cash bequests. Almost every American synagogue of the time was favored. (Conspicuously absent was Beth

Elohim, Charleston's Reform synagogue.) On the list were
Jewish day schools, Catholic and Protestant organizations, civic
institutions such as a fireman's organization. He established a
public park in Newport, still in use to this day. Touro also left
money to orphan homes for boys and girls and almshouses. He
helped libraries and hospitals. Finally, in the Will's last bequest
to an organization, he left $10,000 to the synagogue at Newport
to pay a reader and keep up the cemetery. This was to become
Touro Synagogue, the oldest existing synagogue structure in the
United States.

Giving and helping were part of Touro's life. He endowed
many institutions during his lifetime, and upon his death, the
sheer volume of his beneficiaries outstripped anything done by
any one person up to the middle of the 19th century. His example was to be followed by not only Jews but by all Americans.

Touro was buried in Newport, the city of his birth, next to
the other members of his family. It was a request he had set
down in his will. Aside from the name Touro being associated
with the old synagogue, the street running alongside it also
bears the family name. The funds he bequeathed for the upkeep
of this shrine to American Jewry are still administered in trust
by the city of Newport.

On December 4, 1943, in his adopted city of New Orleans,
the Liberty ship *Judah Touro* was launched to serve as a military tanker during World War II. America had not forgotten this
benefactor though he had died almost 100 years earlier. His
government gave him a further honor. The synagogue where his
father has served as religious leader, now known as the Touro
synagogue, was designated as a National Religious Shrine on
August 31, 1946.

The Louisiana State Capital at Baton Rouge boasts a sculp-
tured panel dedicated to him, while Tulane University awards
gold medals that he established in 1848.

The historic cemetery in Newport where the Touros are
buried contains the graves of early American Jews.

Longfellow's famous poem, "The Jewish Cemetery at Newport," memorializes them:

"The names upon their monuments are strange,
Of foreign accents and of different climes,
Alvarez and Rivera interchange
With Abraham and Jacob of old times."

Judah Touro's gravestone rests among these old stones. His is but one among other early Jews who helped shape America. His stone contains a short tribute to this important benefactor: "The last of his name, he inscribed it in the book of philanthropy, to be remembered forever."

Despite glowing descriptions of the man, Touro was like most people, made up of many facets. Some called him eccentric, indecisive, difficult, peculiar and strange. He had to be pushed in the right direction. But once shown the way, he dispensed charity as no one before him had ever done in America. His landmark will was a model for others to follow.

Portrait of Judah Touro, photograph © John T. Hopf

Exterior, Newport Synagogue, photo © John T. Hopf

Dedication Plaque, Newport Synagogue. Photo © John T Hopf

ISAAC LEESER

*"It will ... appear that no matter how careless the Jews
may be in appearance to their religion, in the eyes of
those who know them not, there is, ... a deep feeling of
attachment to the law of God ... which will at some time
... produce ample fruits of godliness."*
                                        Isaac Leeser

Before 1840, America had no ordained rabbis. Lay leaders
or hazzans occupied all pulpits in American synagogues. These
were men who, because of interest, training or spiritual obliga-
tion, assumed the responsibility of caring for the religious and
educational needs of their congregants. Many were called
Ministers. Some were outstanding: Gershom Mendes Seixas,
the "Patriot Rabbi" of the American Revolution, led New
York's Shearith Israel congregation for decades; Manuel Nuñes
Carvalho served congregations in New York, Charleston,
Philadelphia and Barbados. Both men were well-known early-
American hazzans.

Of them all, Isaac Lesser was the most influential and sig-
nificant. His work extended well beyond the borders of his
Philadelphia congregation, reaching all corners of the United
States. He was a Jewish missionary, an advocate for the spread

of Judaism to every city of his adopted country. He took an active interest in Jewish education, publications, and helped found new synagogues wherever there were families enough to form a community. He was responsible for translating and publishing the first Hebrew bible in English and translated and printed both Sephardic and Ashkenazic versions of prayer books in English for daily synagogue use. Leeser even extended his interest to include printing children's books in English.

All this work might be enough for any one person in a lifetime, but Leeser was also founder and editor of "The Occident," America's most important Jewish publication before the Civil War. He organized the first Jewish Publication Society, America's first theological seminary, and countless other societies - all of which preceded American Jewry's 20th century genius for the institution of communal organizations.

Isaac Leeser was born in Germany in 1806. He studied with rabbis in the city of Muenster. His teachers opposed the Reform movement, which was gaining great acceptance throughout Germany. His education was classic Orthodox, but before he could be ordained, he emigrated to the United States. It was 1824 and Leeser was 18 years old.

Settling in Richmond, Virginia, where he worked at an uncle's store, Leeser became adept in English even while continuing to read and learn about Judaism. Within five years, his mastery of the English language was good enough that he prepared tracts defending Jews against ethnic attacks. Some of them were published in "The Richmond Whig."

His articles were republished in newspapers in other American cities. They attracted favorable attention in Jewish communities. As a consequence, in 1829 this 23-year old of German origin was called on to become the Hazzan of Philadelphia's Mikveh Israel synagogue. It was one of the oldest Jewish communities in the United States and the home of one of the most important and influential congregations in America. Mikveh Israel adhered to the Sephardic ritual. Despite the fact that Leeser was German, this prestigious congregation saw something special in the young man.

Congregation Mikveh Israel was not to be disappointed. Although not a trained or ordained rabbi, Isaac Leeser rose to become one of the most respected religious leaders in the United States, always addressed respectfully as Reverend and Minister.

Through his pulpit in Philadelphia, he was in a position to transform American Jewry for the next four decades. Although he was Ashkenazic, and trained in the Ashkenazic traditions, he would be identified with America's Sephardic community.

Leeser brought to his pulpit two concepts new to American Judaism. First, he consciously worked to combine his religion and his love for America. He accomplished this by introducing English into his sermons. He translated traditional prayer books and the Hebrew bible into English. Then, he brought good basic Jewish education to all American Jews, especially the children. Leeser also understood the need for higher rabbinic education in order to insure a competent rabbinate for the future. He helped to establish institutions that would provide that education.

From the first day he arrived in America, Leeser was determined to become 100 percent American. He quickly buried his European origins. One of his main goals was to help all immigrant Jews in America do the same. He was a strong defender of Anglo-Saxon culture and America's system of democracy and its civil liberties. He exhorted German immigrants to shed their old ways and adopt America completely, without reservations. Leeser even brought this campaign to the religious service by insisting on the use of English for sermons. He was the first in an Orthodox congregation in America to do so regularly.

Reading through Leeser's diaries, one must be impressed by his proficiency in English. Considering his native language was German and that he arrived in America in early adulthood, Leeser wrote clearly, taking into account the literary style of his day.

In the spring of 1843, he began publishing "The Occident." It was America's first successful Jewish publication with a general circulation. (Twenty years earlier, a New York publication called "The Jew" had a short, unsuccessful life.)

"The Occident" was to be Leeser's base for his connection with Jews throughout the United States. The paper gave Leeser access to American Jews in small cities and towns as well as the great urban areas. He wrote about Judaism as he believed it should be practiced in the New World. He was also the paper's editor, publisher, accountant and, when he was low on funds, one of its typesetters.

Leeser set down the principles of "The Occident" in its first issue. He would be dedicated to *"whatever can advance the cause of our religion, and of promoting the true interests of that religion which has made this religion its profession." He would, he said, prefer original articles, but would if necessary, "...resort to publications which are not generally accessible, or furnish translations from Hebrew, French and German works."*

Leeser's choice of the year 1843 to inaugurate "The Occident" was fortunate. German Jewish immigrants were pouring into America at a much greater rate than at any time in its history. By 1860, there would be 150,000 Jews in the United States, ten times the number only 20 years earlier. For many of the newcomers, "The Occident" would be their only exposure to news and events of American and international Jewry. Within its pages, they could learn of the important issues facing them in the middle of the 19th century even as they learned to read English.

Encouraged by the success of "The Occident," Rabbi Isaac Mayer Wise, Leeser's opposite in the Reform camp, began his own publication, "The Israelite." Leeser and Wise often struggled over the emergence of Reform Judaism, but they respected one another. On many occasions, Leeser used "The Occident" to defend Wise's right to advocate his position. To the credit of both of these talented men, each sought to unite the Jewish people, not split them.

Three months before the Civil War began, Leeser became embroiled in the debates that swirled around slavery. On January 4, 1861 Rabbi Morris Jacob Raphall of New York lectured at B'nai Jeshurun in defense of slavery. In an article appearing in "The Occident," Leeser defended Raphall. It was to haunt him in later years when he was accused of being pro-Southern and a secessionist. His role in this affair is puzzling, since he tried to keep clear of supporting either North or South during the War.

During his years at Mikveh Israel, Leeser published America's first primer for children in Hebrew. He also translated the Bible from Hebrew to English. He was the first person to do so in America. It took him 17 years to complete the work.

In 1848, Leeser published the first English translation of the Sephardic prayer book. Almost 100 years later, in 1941, Rabbi David de Sola Pool of New York's Shearith Israel congregation, prepared another Sephardic prayer book, also using English and Hebrew. In his forward to that Siddur, Dr. de Sola Pool credits Leeser's version, noting that it was out of print, requiring a new prayer book for use among America's Sephardim.

This busy man also founded the first Hebrew High School, the Jewish Publication Society, Maimonides College and, in the year before his death, the first American Jewish rabbinical school. But that's not all. Leeser also organized the first American Association of Jewish Congregations. He traveled tirelessly across America, inaugurating new synagogues, visiting congregations, and encouraging small communities to organize. He was a one-man publicist for his American brand of Judaism: a Jewish drumbeater.

One of his great achievements was the positive influence he exerted upon Judah Touro, the New Orleans philanthropist. Leeser restored to Touro his Jewish awareness, convincing him that his vast wealth should be distributed among the synagogues and other Jewish institutions in America. Before he met Leeser, Touro gave very little to Jewish organizations and did not lead a Jewish life. Touro returned to Judaism before his death.

Morris U. Schappes, editor of "Documentary History of the Jews in the United States," quotes Leeser as saying:

"And it is a pleasing reflection that in making his will, Mr. Touro remembered nearly all the objects of public benificence which we had brought to his attention as editor during the last ten years."

In 1850, Lesser officiated at the consecration of a synagogue building in New Orleans that had been purchased by Judah Touro and given to Congregation Nefuzoth Yehudah as a gift. Today, Nefuzoth Israel is known as the Touro Synagogue.

Because of his newspaper, his travels and the influence he forged through the organizations he founded, Leeser was at the forefront of the issues of the day, from anti-Semitism to the growing strength of Reform. He was called upon to officiate at federal, state and municipal events. His influence was to reach into the decade of the Civil War.

Leeser addressed himself to General Ulysses S. Grant's infamous Order No. 11, which expelled Jewish traders from Tennessee during the Civil War. Grant gave the reason that Jewish traders were engaged in smuggling and trading with the enemy. Leeser responded with the longest article ever to appear by him in "The Occident," which attacked the "adventurers" who seek illicit gain.

He joined in the "Chaplaincy Controversy." During the Civil War, Jews were not permitted to have Chaplains attached to military units, as did Catholics and Protestants. Rabbi David Einhorn and others petitioned the Army for the right to such a privilege. Leeser fought for this right more on humanitarian grounds than as a matter of equality. He personally volunteered for chaplaincy services in military hospitals, to stand beside

Jewish soldiers in need.

Leeser was so distressed when he heard of Lincoln's assassination that he was unable to comment immediately. He noted later that Lincoln's kindness and understanding during the affair of Grant's Order No. 11 and the chaplain controversy spoke for his greatness.

Despite these positions, Leeser was often condemned as a pro-Southern secessionist, which he very well may have been. As we have seen, he did spend his first five years in America in Richmond. He had many friends and relatives in the South. He traveled extensively throughout the region before the War, helping to organize its religious life. He may have been emotionally unable to condemn people with whom he had such close contact over the decades, but he was also a citizen and product of the North.

Leeser had the same pangs of loyalty to North and South that Major Alfred Mordecai must have felt. That West Point graduate and career soldier was also a native North Carolinian. Mordecai solved his problem by resigning his commission in the Union army and refusing offers from the south. He finally settled in Philadelphia during the War, teaching mathematics.

Leeser followed the same course as Mordecai. He refused to get involved in politics or condemn either side in the War. His personal position was that Jews should become involved in politics, not as Jews collectively, but as individuals. The situation was difficult for him, since he was personally unable to justify or condemn either side. Despite Leeser's pro-Southern feelings, "The Occident" reflects the scrupulous neutrality which Lesser affected throughout the War.

Leeser's conduct was not unusual. Scholars have noted that the minutes of many synagogues during the Civil War are oddly lacking any mention of the bloody conflict raging around them. The synagogues of Baltimore, a border city close to some of the fiercest battles of the War, reflect little notice of the monumental struggle of which every Jew in that city had to be keenly aware.

The Reverend James K. Gutheim, spiritual leader of Touro Synagogue in New Orleans, was also a man with extensive contacts in the North. He might have summed up the feelings of both Northern and Southern rabbis when he said it was not *"the province of the pulpit to discuss the political questions of the day and to point out the course to be pursued."*

At one point, a highly respected member of Philadelphia's Jewish community berated Leeser publicly for his pro-South leanings. The man warned Leeser that he would be put on a list of suspected subversives. So shaken was Leeser that he appealed to Alexander Henry, mayor of Philadelphia, to be apprised of such a document. Mayor Henry advised him that no such list existed, then went on to assure him that at no time had anyone any doubts as to Leeser's loyalty.

The reality is that Leeser was torn between the conflict, which encompassed practical and idealistic issues, and his personal knowledge of America and intimate association with its Jews. Of all America's rabbis, he was probably the best known. His work for American Judaism, his personal contact with the country's rabbis and their congregants, afforded him great notoriety. So his loyalties, real or imagined, must have been the subject of great interest. Doubtless, many American Jews had erroneous views of where this man stood in the Civil War.

When the War was over, he continued his work in the South. He helped to unite Southern Jewry with the North. He walked through the battlefields, noting places where the Jewish dead was buried. He worked to heal the wounds of that fratricidal war. But the controversy surrounding his Pro-Southern leanings continued even after his death. In his eulogy, Charleston's Reform congregation Beth Elohim stated, *"As Southerners, we grieve over the loss of a bold defender of our rights."*

Unfortunately for Leeser, even before his controversial War years, his congregation did not share his zeal for his work with American Jewry. In 1850, Leeser lost his position at Mikveh

Israel to his Hazzan, Sabato Morais. This Italian rabbi would go on to continue the work started by Leeser. Morais would also translate, publish and become one of the moving forces behind Conservative Jewry in America, as one of the founders of the Jewish Theological Seminary.

In 1858, some of Leeser's admirers formed Congregation Beth El Emeth, where, as Hazzan, he spent the last days of his long career. He died in Philadelphia in 1868.

Many words define Isaac Leeser: energetic, devoted, and dedicated. He was a man with foresight who saw how immigrants from many places could be turned into dedicated Jews and Americans simultaneously. He was a tireless advocate of American Jewry's place in this growing country. More than a missionary for Judaism, he was its publicist. The seeds he planted for Jewish education, awareness and organization bore fruit for subsequent generations.

As with almost every other person in this book, Isaac Leeser felt comfortable with his religion, his love for his country and its institutions. He understood that loyalty to one did not preclude loyalty to the other.

Every rabbi who works with his congregation to instruct them, or who writes in newsletters and journals for the Jewish public, or heads communal organizations, or publishes books of Jewish interest, or speaks out to protest injustice, or encourages the practice of the Jewish religion, is the spiritual child of the remarkable Isaac Leeser.

Portrait of Isaac Leeser, National Museum of American Jewish
History, Philadelphia

ERNESTINE L. ROSE

" ... on human rights and freedom - on a subject that is self-evident as two and two make four, there is no need of any written authority."

Ernestine L. Rose

Immigrants to America not only exchanged countries and adopted new lifestyles, they often assumed new names, and ideals and goals they may never have dreamed of achieving. Such a person was Sismondi Potowski. She was the daughter of the rabbi of the Polish hamlet of Pyeterkow.

Born in 1810 and raised studying scripture in a strict Orthodox environment, Sismondi could speak and read Hebrew. As a young teenager, she already began creating disturbances by advocating woman's equality and questioning the truth of Jewish law concerning the role of women in society. Breaking completely with 19th century social constrictions at 16, she hauled her father into the law courts after the death of her wealthy mother. The issue turned upon Sismondi's legitimate share of her mother's estate. After winning her lawsuit, she traveled throughout Poland, Russia and Western Europe. She became self-sufficient by living off the proceeds of a household deodorant she invented.

Hailed as a prodigy, exaggerated descriptions of Sismondi's travels in Europe recount meetings with royalty, complete with descriptions of how she berated them for social injustice within their countries. Assuming this to be true, she had to have been a remarkable woman, since at the time she was barely out of her teens and a woman alone.

There may have been some basis for these stories. When she arrived in Germany, she was able to appeal to the King to have certain immigration disabilities personally waived for her.

While traveling in England in 1832, she became attracted to Utopian Socialism, becoming a disciple of Robert Own, its founder. In 1835, she married an Englishman, William Rose. He was an atheist, a fellow socialist and an abolitionist. The couple left for the United States the following year.

Wasting no time in her newly adopted country, this dynamic woman began a distinguished career of social activism. She was to become respected and world famous by her new name, Ernestine L. Rose. Her work preceded the Woman's Rights movement, as we know it today, by a century. She became a force not only for sexual equality, but also for universal justice.

Arriving in New York City in 1836, Ernestine Rose stepped into a society not much different from Europe's, with respect to the treatment of women. In this new culture, where equality was quickly granted to all immigrants of different religions and national origins, women did not benefit from American egalitarianism. They were, in fact, expected to perform all the grueling work of the frontier settler without the benefits of the equality male immigrants enjoyed.

Rose quickly understood her role in American society. Soon after arriving in New York, she petitioned the state legislature for the repeal of laws creating civil disabilities for women. She was faced with almost complete indifference at first. It was a fight that took almost a decade to win. Even with this victory, she was unable to open all the locked doors that barred women's freedom. But she was instrumental in having the New York legislature enact the country's first law permitting a woman to hold real property in her own name instead of that of her spouse, parent or guardian.

It was a world in which a married woman was legally considered her husband's chattel. A woman could not sue unless her husband consented to give her that right; nor could she have complete control of her children. All these legal rights belonged to her spouse. Ernestine Rose was to labor more than three decades in the United States, fighting these legal principles and overturning these injustices.

What was remarkable about this extraordinary woman was that despite the fact she was often characterized as a "Polish Jewess," spoke English with an accent and was a woman in a man's world, she drew large, enthusiastic crowds at all of her lectures around the United States. She was a magnetic speaker. Contemporary accounts describe her as attractive, animated, witty, logical and, above all, impressive. She lectured on the science of government, atheism, slavery, women's right to education, women's rights generally, and universal equality.

It did not take long for Ernestine Rose to become one of the most dynamic and sought-after women speakers on America's lecture circuit. She won a reputation as "The Queen of the Platform." As a delegate to the first National Women's Rights Convention, in Massachusetts in 1850, she joined forces with the great social activists of the time: Lucretia Mott, William Lloyd Garrison and Lucy Stone. Characteristically, she wasted little time getting to work. Assigned to working committees, Rose presented the most important report at the convention, to the acclamation of the delegates.

Rose continued to be active at Women's Rights conventions over the years. When men confronted her with quotes from the bible to *"prove"* women's inferior status, she delivered a famous speech that was then published in pamphlet form and widely circulated around the country:

"Wherever human rights are claimed for man, moral consistency points to equal rights for women."

In her address, she pointed out that men have stated:

"... (assuming) the corruption of the present state of politics. It is represented to be in so low and degraded a condition that no one can enter the political arena without contamination, and therefore a woman must be kept from its very atmosphere."

She countered that argument with the obvious answer: Let women enter politics; they will then clean up the pigsties sullied by corrupt legislators.

Her intimate knowledge of the bible allowed her to call up passages at will to be used against her detractors. She forcefully argued that any biblical authority espousing the denial of female equal rights was invalid. There was no need to point to any written authority for the proposition that people were equal. Equality was a basic fact, a truism that was as much a part of the universe as nature's laws.

In 1861, the national work of women's rights was suspended by the Civil War. But Ernestine Rose did not stop working for justice. She, Susan B. Anthony, Elizabeth Stanton and others founded and organized the Women's National Loyal League. They petitioned President Lincoln to emancipate slaves at an early stage of the Civil War. Rose was also closely associated with the anti-slave agitator, Stephan Douglass, by calling for the immediate and legal abolition of slavery.

At the close of the War, she focused her attention westward. Women's suffrage had its greatest early successes in America's western pioneering communities. It was here in the newly settled towns west of the Mississippi that Ernestine Rose worked tirelessly to bring the principles of women's suffrage. Wyoming was the first state to grant this right, in 1869.

In that same year, she reluctantly retired from public life. Decades of hard work, long hours of traveling and selfless devotion to the causes she championed, had ruined her health. She returned to England, to live as an invalid for the remainder of her life. Divorced from her husband, she settled in Brighton, England, where she died in 1892. Twenty-eight years after her death, the United States passed the 19th Amendment, guaranteeing suffrage to all of America's women.

Today, Ernestine L. Rose is mostly forgotten. She nevertheless continues to live on in spirit, through those who followed her: Gloria Steinhem, Betty Friedan and Bella Abzug. Contemporary accounts of this tireless lady have described her variously as holding odd and non-conformist religious views. On the other hand, she was also characterized as a religious Jew, who insisted on following the *"strict observation of all the rites and ceremonies of the Jewish faith."*

Perhaps there was a bit of truth to both of these descriptions. Her early religious training must have influenced her. It showed in her burning zeal for social justice and equality for everyone; in her uncanny and easy ability to quote pertinent bible passages from memory during open public debates.

Because of her Jewish roots, Rose had to face public approbation during her public life. She was often described as the "Jewess" or the "Polish Jewess." Newspapers and magazines never let her forget her religion, her Polish origin or her "inferior" status as a woman.

There are no accounts that she ever repudiated her Jewish heritage or her past. She remained a Jew and always a respected equal of her colleagues and other contemporaries. Her fame and public exposure must have been a credit to the Jewish community at large. In her work and ideals, she exemplified the Jewish concept that all human beings should live in dignity.

Ernestine L. Rose does not deserve to be forgotten. In her

society, women enjoyed no civil rights. She refused to accept that fact. She joined with others to change this injustice. The fight she began never ended for her, not even after the passage of the 19th Amendment. It continues to this day, as does her spirit.

Portrait of Ernestine L. Rose, Schlesinger Library

JUDAH P. BENJAMIN

"His career ... is not likely to be repeated with all the fascination of a brilliantly narrated romance."
The Morning Telegraph, London, England, 1884

In all of America's history, Judah P. Benjamin was probably the country's most politically powerful Jew. But few Americans are aware of that fact.

In 1852 as Senator from Louisiana, Benjamin became the first acknowledged Jew to sit in that chamber. Although Florida's David Levy Yulee preceded him, Yulee publicly denounced his religion, making up the story that he was really the son of a Moroccan prince.

Benjamin was the first Jew to be considered for a seat on the United States Supreme Court. President Millard Fillmore offered him that honor in 1852. Benjamin rejected the nomination. When an Ambassadorship to Spain was offered, he spurned that, too. He was one of America's great lawyers, participating in some of the most significant cases of his time. When he resigned from his Senate seat on the eve of the Civil

War, his colleagues were genuinely sorry to see him leave, for his speeches were masterpieces of logic, professionally delivered with great oratory. His farewell address to the Senate in 1861 was considered one of the finest made before that body.

Benjamin became alternately the first American Jewish Secretary of Justice, War and State when he assumed those three cabinet posts for the Confederacy. It was he who was the main confidant and advisor of Confederate President Jefferson Davis, all through the Civil War.

Today's Southerners revere men like Stonewall Jackson, Robert E. Lee and Jefferson Davis. But Judah P. Benjamin, the man who represented the South's political power to the world at large, is merely a footnote in American history.

There are reasons for his relative obscurity. First, Benjamin destroyed his personal papers at the end of the Civil War. Historians have little material to study in order to understand the reasons for many of his actions. Much of what we do know comes from impersonal government communiqués, newspaper reports or observations by his contemporaries, among them anti-Semites and political rivals.

Even Jefferson Davis, who daily relied on Benjamin's counsel during the Civil War, makes only two references to him in his multi-volume memoirs, "The Rise and Fall of the Confederate Government." One wonders why Davis makes so little note of this extraordinary man, who was so devoted to him. They dined almost daily at Jefferson's Confederate White House. Their offices were close to one another at Confederate Headquarters. Davis depended so heavily upon Benjamin's advice, in fact, that Benjamin came to be known as "The Brains of the Confederacy."

On many occasions, Benjamin was the President's voice, advising Southerners of bad news and unpopular new laws. He did this to spare the President's image and prevent political groundswells against him.

Civil War historians agree that Jefferson Davis was a man

who did not enjoy sharing power. He tended to have people about him whom he could control, and would not try to usurp him. It may have been that Davis purposely underwrote Benjamin. We may never know. If that is true, however, Benjamin didn't seem to care. John George Witt, Benjamin's English executor, said of him, *"When he died, he did not leave behind him a half dozen pieces of paper."*

Another reason for Benjamin's relative obscurity may be the bitterness that developed among Southerners after their defeat. It grew into hatred for Blacks, Jews and the Northern occupiers. Christian soldiers were their logical heroes, not a Jewish outsider like Judah P. Benjamin.

Unlike Uriah P. Levy, Benjamin did not consciously set out to cut a path for other Jews. He was not a member of the Jewish community and, as far as is known, he engaged in no Jewish activities after attaining adulthood. But the Christian world never let Benjamin forget his Jewish roots: through national exposure, Benjamin was America's most visible Jew in the years before and during the Civil War.

Life for this remarkable man began in 1811 on the island of St. Croix, in the Virgin Islands. At the time, St. Croix was not an American possession. Benjamin's father was English and he never completely surrendered his claim to English Citizenship - an act that would be his salvation half a century later.

He was descended from the distinguished Sephardic families of De Leon and Mendes. In 1813, his family moved to North Carolina. Earning a living there was difficult, however, and by 1823 Philip Benjamin, Judah's father, decided to try his luck in the city of Charleston, South Carolina.

Charleston was one of America's most important cities and home to the largest and most affluent Jewish community in North America. Philip and Rebecca Benjamin and their family settled down to a life of minor merchants with a minimal income. Philip Benjamin joined Congregation Beth Elohim and allied himself with the faction agitating for its religious reform.

In 1824, the congregation made some changes in the service, such as the use of English.

Philip Benjamin was such a religious rebel, however, he was unable to conform his radical ideas to the newly organized congregation. In 1827 he was expelled from Beth Elohim for keeping his shop open on the Sabbath.

Beth Elohim eventually became America's first Reform synagogue, and the accompanying excitement could not have failed to impress young Judah.

It was in Charleston during the early years of the 19th century that the bitter struggle between Orthodoxy and religion's change began. Judah P. Benjamin's father was just one of its players. That early strife, which at the time may have seemed just a local conflict, has stalked American Jewry to the present.

Judah and Philip Benjamin take their place in American and Jewish history as significant secessionists and factionalists. First Philip, the father, and others of his synagogue broke away from Orthodoxy to follow a new ritual. Such action today would be commonplace. At that time, the effect was shattering. Then, the son followed the father: he helped to lead Southern states away from the Union. Philip's rebellion was successful; Judah's ended in defeat.

Because the records of Beth Elohim were destroyed by fire, there is no verification that Judah was Bar Mitzvah or confirmed at Beth Elohim. It would not be too presumptuous to assume he was. Philip was a rebel, but he cared for the religion of his fathers. He studied Torah and his house was filled with all sorts of books, including those of the Jews. Philip and Rebecca saw to it that young Judah attended the Hebrew Orphan Society School, in Charleston.

Benjamin's memory was prodigious. His comprehension of books, once read, was impressive. Moses Lopez, a member of Charleston's Jewish community, offered to educate this young marvel. Rebecca Benjamin, the impoverished descendant of Sephardic Grandees, readily agreed: the offer included Yale

Law School, the temple of America's elite. Eli Evans, Judah Benjamin's biographer, tells us that when she packed Judah's clothes for New Haven, Rebecca Benjamin included a Hebrew prayer book.

Judah Benjamin's formal contact with his Jewishness ended in 1825, the year he left for Yale. To his credit, he never disavowed his religion. He married a New Orleans Creole Catholic of the establishment and lived among Christians the rest of his life. For all his power, conversion might have eliminated that untidy corner of his political life. He might have avoided some of the vile epithets that would be flung at him.

When only 14, Judah Benjamin presented himself for enrollment at America's most prestigious institute of learning. He was one of the first Jews to attend Yale and for the two years he was there, the only one. Before the Civil War, the Southern elite sent their sons to be educated at Yale. Fully 25-percent of the student body was from the South. The remainder was the cream of northern society. This Jewish son of poor immigrants must have felt the outsider.

During his two years at Yale, Benjamin excelled academically. But he left under circumstances that have never been fully explained. He was not expelled. He left voluntarily. Unsubstantiated charges of theft were to follow him for the rest of his life. Only one thing is clear: there is no record why he left Yale other than his letter of resignation, and that contains no explanation.

Benjamin did not return to Charleston. Instead, at 16, he chose the raw frontier community of New Orleans in the newly purchased territory of Louisiana. He set out to become a lawyer and quickly made a name for himself with his brilliance.

Within 10 years of his arrival, New Orleans had doubled in size, becoming a cosmopolitan, French-oriented city. It was the perfect dream for a fledgling lawyer and, as with other frontier cities, people did not look at who you were or where you came from. Everyone came from some other place.

Benjamin was an opportunist. He made himself the perfect Southerner: he married Natalie St. Martin, a product of the Creole aristocracy; established strong political ties; and fit into the Southern attitude by becoming a plantation and slave-owner. He wrote legal textbooks, was one of America's leading lawyers in the courtroom and, eventually, the Senator from Louisiana.

When the Civil War began, Benjamin was the South's leading trial lawyer in addition to being an ex-U.S. senator. He was the perfect selection for a leadership position with the seceding states. He represented the South, first as Attorney General, then Secretary of War. Finally, he became Secretary of State, the post he held for most of the War.

As the South's stunning early victories gave way to a series of heartbreaking defeats, opposition to Benjamin arose. Southern President Jefferson Davis stood by his Secretary of State. Though he was not a military man, Benjamin was blamed for every defeat in the field. To add to his woes, Benjamin assumed the position of the President's spokesman. It fell to him to advise Southerners of the new rules and regulations restricting their lives, much of which resulted from blockades and loss of access to manufacturing markets. Civilians were deprived of food, clothing and medicine and to many, Judah P. Benjamin was to blame.

In 1864, aware of the South's precarious position, Benjamin proposed a drastic solution to increase the size of its dwindling army: emancipation of its slaves. Would Davis agree? With the fall of Atlanta in September 1864, the South's military situation became desperate. Davis might consider. In November, Davis addressed the Confederate Congress in his annual message to them. Judah P. Benjamin wrote the speech.

Davis advised his Congress there would have to be adjustments with respect to the legal status of slaves. The groundwork was being laid. *"The slaves would have to join the Confederate forces and fight,"* he said.

On February 5, 1865, over 10,000 people crammed into a church and its immediate environs off Richmond's Capitol Square. After several speeches by Davis and other Confederate dignitaries, Benjamin rose to address the crowd. He had not delivered any major speech since his Senate resignation. He was testing the waters for the President. Benjamin was now publicly advocating emancipation, something he had considered for years. Robert E. Lee needed more troops; Benjamin was trying to get them. Despite a brilliant speech, accepted with applause and assent, Benjamin failed to convince the majority of his fellow southerners that slaves should be armed.

Weeks later, the Confederate Senate came very close to passing a resolution of no confidence against their Secretary of State. Benjamin offered his resignation to Davis, who refused it. The Confederate Congress may have hated Benjamin, but Davis stood by his loyal cabinet member. Then, marshalling his political power, Davis bulled through Congress a slave enlistment act with no teeth. Lee's desperate requests for additional manpower went unanswered. The end was near. Less than two months later, Robert E. Lee surrendered his sword to General Grant at Appomattox.

At War's end, leading members of the Confederate government were open to the serious charge of treason. Some Northern political leaders blamed Abraham Lincoln's assassination on Jefferson Davis and his cabinet. They were convinced officials in Richmond hatched the plot. Rewards were placed on the heads of Davis and others, including Benjamin.

In a letter written to one of his sisters, Benjamin expressed the wish never to be caught alive. Northern politicians were making up lists of Confederate leaders they planned to swing from a tree. Benjamin's name was on every one of them. A student of history, he would have surely known that under similar circumstances, Jews had fared poorly in the past. This tough-minded, quick-witted man made his escape while the North, furious at the assassination of its President, was calling for vengeance and hangings of those they thought to be responsible.

He made his way out through Florida. After a journey made up of pure adventure, he passed through the Florida Keys to the British island of Bimini in the Bahamas. From there, he sailed to London. His escape had been successful.

Amazingly, he started a new life at age 54 as an English Barrister. He became one of the ablest in the British Isles. His long dormant claim to English citizenship permitted him to qualify for the Bar. He was to become Queen's Counsel and go on to write a book on the Law of Sales which became a classic.

Benjamin could have returned to the United States when general amnesty was later declared. Many Southern leaders who had fled to England, Canada and Mexico did return. Benjamin and a few others chose to remain abroad.

Unlike most of the dozen American Jews presented in this book, Benjamin did not unite his religion with his love for his country. Yet there is no doubt of his importance in American history and the fact that he was always identified as Jewish. He never converted or denounced his Judaism, as did David Levy Yulee of Florida.

Another man in the British Isles, also a descendant of Spanish and Portuguese Jews and Benjamin's contemporary, held power as Prime Minister of England. In a country which did not permit Jews to hold any public office, Benjamin Disraeli, a Jewish convert to the Anglican Church, was one of the world's most powerful men.

There are uncanny similarities in the lives of Disraeli and Benjamin. Both families were descended from Sephardic Jews, refugees from Iberia. Both men were of immigrant families. Disraeli's came to England from Turkey by way of Italy; Benjamin's from St. Croix by way of St. Eustatius and London. The fathers of both men were renegades in their synagogues. Isaac Disraeli refused to follow the rules of his English congregation, resigned and had young Benjamin converted to the

Anglican Church. Judah's father was one of the founders of America's first Reform congregation.

Although they were outsiders, Disraeli and Benjamin married women who were within the establishment, which helped them in their careers. Both men had highly visible first careers before they ascended to power: Benjamin was a well-known lawyer; Disraeli a writer of novels. Both were known for their keen minds, sharp wit and oratory talents. Finally, Disraeli and Benjamin each rose to political power by first attaining legislative seats, in Parliament and the Senate, respectively.

The similarity ends there. Disraeli wielded great power both in England and abroad. He was elevated to the Peerage, as the Earl of Beaconsfield, for his services to the Crown. Benjamin received no rewards for his work on behalf of the Confederacy.

The paths of these two extraordinary men would meet in England when Disraeli would come to Judah Benjamin's aid. Disraeli's biographer confirms the fact that it was he who assisted Benjamin in his efforts to become a Barrister. In 1870, Disraeli again helped obtain the designation of Queen's Counselor for Benjamin. It was then, as it is today, a highly prestigious title in the English legal profession.

Disraeli's ticket to power was the legal effect of his conversion. It was what qualified him for elected office. To his death, however, he was an outsider among the English upper class, much as Benjamin had been in his environment.

Bitterness after the South's defeat, at Jews, Blacks, and Northerners, may have distorted much of Benjamin's role. But this feeling may not necessarily have been universal while Benjamin held power. He proved that a Jew could hold important political power in America without resorting to conversion or expressing publicly that his religion was an impossible obstacle that could never be overcome.

Not until 1906, when President Theodore Roosevelt appointed Oscar Straus as Secretary of Commerce and Labor, did America have another Jewish cabinet member. In 1916,

President Woodrow Wilson nominated the first Jewish Supreme Court judge, Louis D. Brandeis. It was 65 years after Benjamin had rejected his nomination. And it took more than a century for another Jewish immigrant to America, Henry Kissinger, to become Secretary of State.

By 1865, Judah P. Benjamin either held all of these offices or could have held them. Despite his obvious talents, it may be that he is not honored among American Jews because he did not identify with them and was a leader of the Confederacy. His early espousal of slavery was not popular with most Jews.

How does one explain that Disraeli was recognized as an honored personage amongst world Jewry, despite his conversion? Disraeli's government was the world's most powerful and respected, while Judah Benjamin was an outcast who represented an unpopular cause and a weak nation. There is an adage, "winners write history." And it was not Disraeli who converted willingly, but the act of his angry father when Disraeli was a boy. As Prime Minister of England or Member of Parliament, Disraeli never hid his origins. In his novels and in his speeches to Parliament, he always acknowledged his ancestry. He associated with and defended Jews, whereas Benjamin never took such positions. There is even evidence that he was negatively obsessed with his ancestry.

Almost 100 years after the Civil War, the United States was engaged in a World War against Germany and Japan. America embarked upon a shipbuilding program for the Armed Forces. These Liberty ships, as they were called, were named for significant Americans. Both Benjamin and Jefferson Davis were honored: each man had a ship named for him. In this odd twist of history, these two comrades-in-arms who had spent so much of the five years of the Civil War together directing the fate and fortunes of the Confederate States of America, would go to war again against a new enemy.

The *Judah P. Benjamin* was designated as ship number 237. The *Jefferson Davis* bore number 238. Fittingly, the Alabama

Drydock and Shipping Company on Pinto Island in Mobile Bay built both ships. They left the yard in August 1942, among the earliest of the thousands of military vessels to be put in service during World War II. Both ships survived the War and were scrapped in Washington State in 1961.

Benjamin died in 1884. His wife, Natalie St. Martin, buried him in a Catholic cemetery in Paris. The plot in which he lies belongs to the in-laws of his daughter Ninette. His gravestone reads "Philippe Benjamin," the name by which his wife always addressed him. There is no evidence that he ever converted to Catholicism.

His gravesite went unnoticed until 1938, when the Daughters of the American Confederacy prepared the following inscription and rescued the site from anonymity:

> *"Judah Philip Benjamin*
> *Born St. Thomas West Indies August 6, 1811*
> *Died in Paris May 6 1884*
> *United States Senator from Louisiana*
> *Attorney General, Secretary of War and*
> *Secretary of State of the Confederate States of America*
> *Queen's Counsel London"*

In a newspaper article reporting his death, the writer stated: *"His life was as varied as an eastern tale, and he carved out for himself by his own unaided exertions, not one, but three histories of great and well earned distinction. Inherent in him was the elastic resistance to evil fortune which preserved his ancestors through a succession of exiles and plunderings."*

Thus, appropriately, came to a close the career of one of America's most fascinating and enigmatic public figures.

Portrait of Judah P. Benjamin. National Museum of American
Jewish History, Philadelphia

APPENDICES

Newport Social Club:

(The Jews of Newport banded together to form the first Jewish gentlemen's club in North America. Here are some of the Club's rules and the names of the founders.)

Rules of a Newport club of Jews, November 25, 1761

Rules Necessary to Be Observed At The Club Viz:

First. – The Club is to be held every Wednesday evening during the winter season. The members to be nine in number; and by the majority of votes a chairman to be elected to serve one month only.

Second, - After one month, or four club nights, a new chairman to be elected in the manner aforesaid.

Third. – No person to be admitted as a member of said club without approbation of the members.

Fourth. – Each of the members shall have liberty to invite his friends to the club, well understood, one at a time only.

Fifth. – The hours of club to be from 5 to 10, in the manner following: From 5 to 8 each member is at liberty to divert at cards, and in order to avoid the name of a gaming club, the following restrictions shall be strictly observed, viz: That no member shall presume or offer to play for more than twenty shillings at whist, picquet or any other game besides his club; on proof of gaming for any more, the member or members so offending shall pay the value of four bottles good wines for the use and benefit of the ensuing club night.

Sixth. – At eight of the clock the supper (if ready) to be brought in. At ten the club to be adjusted and paid, and no cards or any other game shall be allowed after supper.

Seventh. – After supper if any of the members have any motion to make relating to the club he must wait till the chairman has just drank some loyal toast.

Eighth. – That none of the members shall ... during... conversation relating to Synagogue affairs, on the forfeit of the value of four bottles good wine for the use as aforesaid.

Ninth. – If any of the members should behave unruly, curse, swear or offer to fight, the chairman shall lay such fine as he sees fit, not exceeding, for each offence, four bottles good wine for the use aforesaid.

Tenth.- If any of the members happen to be sick or absent, by acquainting Mr. Myer with the same, shall be exempt from paying anything towards the club, but if no notice given as aforesaid, shall pay his quota of the supper only.

Eleventh. – If any of the members does not meet at club nights, and can't offer sufficient reason for so doing, the chairman with the members shall determine if he or they are to pay the proportion of the whole club, or the quota of supper only.

Twelfth. – If any of the members neglect coming to club three nights successively without being sick or absent, shall be deemed unwilling, consequently his name shall be erased from the list, and no more to be admitted during the season.

Thirteenth. – Ever[y] member, after signing the articles, and not willing afterwards to conform to the same, his or their names shall be erased out of the list, and no more to be admitted during the season.

In witness thereof the members of said club have signed their respective names the day and year above written.

Moses Lopez, Isaac Polock, Jacob Isaacs, Abr'm Sarzedas, Nap/t. Hart, Moses Levy, Issachar Polock, Naph't. Hart Jr., Jacob Rods. Rivera

Fourteenth. At a club held the 16th day of December, 1761, it is resolved and agreed by the chairman and the majority of all the members that these articles be inserted amongst the rules of said club, viz:

That in case the chairman is not at the club, the secretary, for the time being, shall take his place, and the same obedience shall be paid him as if the chairman was present, and to be invested with equal authority. As also the said secretary is hereby empowered to nominate with the concurrence of the members then present, a secretary to supply his place for the time being; and that every month a secretary shall be elected in the same manner and form as the chairman is elected.

Washington's Letter

(In response to a letter from Newport's Jewish community, George Washington wrote a letter setting forth the American concept of freedom of religion.

In plain words, Washington confirmed the ideals of the American Revolution when he noted that the stock of Abraham would live in peace in the newly-born America.)

To The Hebrew Congregation in New Port Rhode Island

Gentlemen:

While I receive, with much satisfaction, your Address replete with expressions of affection, and esteem; I rejoice in the opportunity of answering you, that I shall always retain a grateful remembrance of the cordial welcome I experienced in my visit to Newport, from all classes of Citizens.

The reflection on the days of difficulty and danger which are past is rendered the more sweet, from a consciousness that they are succeeded by days of uncommon prosperity and security. If we have wisdom to make the best of the advantages with which we are now favored, we cannot fail, under the just administration of a good Government, to become a great and a happy people.

The Citizens of the United States of America have a right to applaud themselves for having given to mankind examples of an enlarged and liberal policy: a policy worthy of imitation. All possess alike liberty of conscience and immunities of citizenship. It is now no more that toleration is spoken of, as if it was by the indulgence of one class of people, that another enjoyed the exercise of their inherent rights. For happily the Government of the United States, which gives to bigotry no sanction, to persecution no assistance, requires only that they who live under its protection should demean themselves as good citizens, in giving it on all occasions their effectual support.

It would be inconsistent with the frankness of my character not to avow that I am pleased with your favorable opinion of my administration, and fervent wishes for my felicity. May the children of the stock of Abraham, who dwell in this land, continue to merit and enjoy the good will of the other Inhabitants, while every one shall sit in safety under his own vine and figtree, and there shall be none to make him afraid. May the father of all mercies scatter light and not darkness in our paths, and make us all in our several vocations useful here, and in his own due time and way everlastingly happy.

G. Washington [signature]

Mordecai Sheftall:

*(In the battle for Savannah, the city fell to British forces.
Mordecai Sheftall was among officers of the Continental Army
that were captured. Because of his reputation as a rebel and
even possibly because of his religion, he was singled out for
special treatment. In this excerpt of his autobiography, he tells
us what it was like to be a captured American officer in
British hands.)*

"The day the British troops, consisting of about three thousand five hundred men, including two battalions of Hessians,
under the command of Lieutenant-Colonel Archibald
Campbell, of the 71st regiment of Highlanders, landed early in
the morning at Brewton Hill, two miles below the town of
Savannah, where they met with very little opposition before
they gained the height. At about three o'clock, P.M., they
entered, and took possession of Savannah, when I endeavored,
with my son Sheftall, to make our escape across Musgrove
Creek…but on our arrival at the creek, after having sustained
a very heavy fire of musketry from the light infantry… during
the time we were crossing the Common, without any injury to
either of us, we found in high water; and my son, not knowing how to swim, and we, with about one hundred and eighty-
six officers and privates, being caught, as it were, in a pen,
and the Highlanders keeping up a constant fire on us, it was
thought advisable to surrender ourselves prisoners…

"…we were marched in files, guarded by the Highlanders
and York volunteers, who had come up before we were
marched… where we saw the greatest part of the army drawn
up. From there, after some time, we were all marched through
the town to the court-house, which was very much crowded,
the greatest part of the officers they had taken being here collected, and indiscriminately put together. I had been here
about two hours, when an officer, who I after wards learned to
be Major Crystie, called for me by name, and ordered me to

follow him, which I did, with my blanket and shirt under my arm, my clothing and my son's, which were in my saddle-bags, having been taken from my horse, so that my wardrobe consisted of what I had on my back.

"On our way to the white guard-house we met with Colonel Campbell, who inquired of the Major who he had got there. On his naming me to him, he desired that I might be well guarded, as I was a very great rebel. The Major obeyed his orders, for, on lodging me in the guard-house, he ordered the sentry to guard me with a drawn bayonet and not to suffer me to go without the reach of it; which orders were strictly complied with until …their Commissary General called for me …he ordered me to give him information of what stores I had in town, and what I had sent out of town, and where. This I declined doing, which made him angry. He asked me if I knew that Charlestown was taken. I told him no. He then called us poor, deluded wretches, and said, "Good God! How are you deluded by your leaders!" When I inquired of him who had taken it, and when he said General Grant, with ten thousand men, and that it had been taken eight or ten days ago, I smiled, and told him it was not so, as I had a letter in my pocket that was wrote in Charlestown but three days ago by my brother. He replied, we had been misinformed. I then retorted that I found they could be misinformed by their leaders as well as we could be deluded by ours. This made him so angry, that when he returned me to the guard-house, he ordered me to be confined amongst the drunken soldiers and Negroes, where I suffered a great deal of abuse, and was threatened to be run through the body, or, as they termed it, skivered by one of the York volunteers, which threat he attempted to put into execution three times during the night, but was prevented by one Sergeant Campbell.

"In this situation I remained two days without a morsel to eat, when a Hessian officer named Zaltman, finding I could talk his language, removed me to his room, and sympathized with me on my situation. He permitted me to send to Mrs.

Minis, who sent me some victuals. He also permitted me to go and see my son, and to let him come and stay with me. He introduced me to Captain Kappel, also a Hessian, who treated me very politely. In this situation I remained until Saturday morning, the 2nd of January, 1779, when ....I met with Captain Stanhope of the Raven sloop of war, who treated me with the most illiberal abuse; and after charging me with having refused the supplying the King's ships with provisions... together with many ill-natured things, ordered me on board the prison-ship, together with my son..."

Thomas Kennedy's 1818 Report to the Legislature of Maryland

Wednesday,
December 9, 1818

On Motion by MR. KENNEDY, Ordered that a committee of three be apponted to consider the justice and expediency of extending to those persons professing the Jewish Religion, the same privileges that are enjoyed by Christians. --Ordered that Messrs. Kennedy, Brackenridge and E.S. Thomas be the said committee.

Monday,
December 21, 1818

Mr. KENNEDY delivers the following Report: -

"The committee appointed to consider the justice and expediency of extending to persons professing the Jewish Religion, the same privileges that are enjoyed by Christians, have taken the same into their serious consideration, and asked leave to report: -

That with respect to the justice of the case submitted to their consideration, your committee think there can be no question, in society, mankind have civil and political duties to perform, but with regard to religion, that is a question which rests, or ought to rest, between man and his creator alone; there is no law can reach the heart – no human tribunal that has a right to take cognizance of this matter..."

Uriah Phillips Levy: Testimony Before Second Court of Inquiry, 1857

(During his 1857 Board of Inquiry, Uriah Levy made a long and dramatic presentation of his life as a sailor, beginning with his decision to run away to sea as a lad, to the most recent events prior to 1857.

Levy was the leading foe of the lash and corporal punishment as discipline aboard U.S. Naval vessels. This excerpt describes his narration of the "Tar Baby" episode in which he punished a cabin boy for insubordination by placing tar and a feather on the boy's bottom. The irony is that Levy chose this punishment to spare the young boy a lifetime reminder of scars the lash would have inflicted. Despite this humane decision, Levy was brought up on charges for dispensing "cruel and unusual" punishment, another example of the anti-Jewish sentiment he had to constantly fight.)

Charge: Scandalous and cruel conduct unbecoming an officer and a gentleman:

Specification: In this, that the said Commander Uriah P. Levy, being then in command of the United States Ship "Vandalia," did on or about the seventh day of July, eighteen hundred and thirty-nine, cause John Thompson, a boy serving on said ship "Vandalia," to be seized to a gun, his trowsers to be let down, and a quantity of tar to be applied to his naked skin, such punishment being highly scandalous and unbecoming the dignity of an officer to inflict, and in violation of the third and thirtieth articles of the first section of the act of Congress entitled "An act for the better government of the Navy of the United States," approved 23rd April 1800 ...

I now propose, Mr. President and gentlemen of the court, to examine the evidence in relation to the treatment of the boy Thompson...

It may be necessary to premise, may it please the court, that this boy Thompson did not only mimic an officer in giving his orders, as was shewn by the testimony of several witnesses, but he was actually in the habit of doing so whenever an occasion presented. No one will deny that such practices are calculated to bring an officer into ridicule and contempt, and thus very materially impair that subordination and good government which ought to exist on board a ship of war, and also to abridge the personal respect which is due to every individual in authority, and yet this mimicry may be classed among the non-enumerated offenses for which the law has provided no specific punishment. It was a new and novel case, calculated, it is true, to lead to unpleasant consequences, but still it was considered by me as a trick, a folly, a boyish misdemeanour. In such light I viewed it, and in such light I noticed it.

I was unwilling to call all hands to punishment and flog the boy on his naked back with a cat [-o' nine tails], for what might possibly be termed a trivial offense; but as a commutation of punishment, I deemed it right, by exposing *him* to ridicule, to satisfy him of the impropriety of ridiculing others. Accordingly, I called the boys together to witness the example to be made of juvenile offenders of this class, had his trowsers taken down, a little tar, on a piece of oakum, dabbed on his bottom, and a few colored feathers from a dead parrot stuck on him to ridicule his mocking propensities, and the whole affair ended in a few minutes. And yet this light and trivial circumstance, originating in jest, not in anger, more as a caution hereafter than punishment for the present, of which nothing was thought of then, nor since, excepting in the humane imagination of the complainant, is magnified into a grave offence, and I am charged with scandalous and cruel conduct and brought before this court to answer such charge.

... If I had not the good fortune to enlist the regard and attachment of all my officers, I was always secure in the confidence, devotion, and attachment of my men.

They were always anxious to remain with me. They were always devoted to me on sea or land. They knew me as the sailor's friend, and their hearts and hands were ever at my disposal and command. *Their* comfort, *their* character, *their* rights, were ever uppermost in my thoughts, and I could have carried my crew at all times in the hottest and most dangerous position of the fight, and I say this without vanity or ostentation, for it is *true*, and therefore I deny that on this occasion there were any manifestations of mutiny or rebellion in my crew.

The complainant in this case has been exceedingly anxious to impart to this trifling affair the most offensive character. If he could only have it said that a man, a white man, was tarred and feathered on board my ship and by my orders, he could create a prejudice and awaken an indignation against me strong enough everywhere to cover me with odium. If he could only blow this *spark* into *flame*, why, he would "feed fat the ancient grudge he bore me." But, may it please the court, it is beyond his power, his ingenuity, to torture this contemptible affair into such an issue; he has a thinking, a discerning, and a sensible court and community to deal with, capable of discriminating and arriving at fair, reasonable, and equitable results in this matter.

...If the spies placed around me to detail any little flaw in my discipline, and then, after a lapse of three years and upwards, to originate charges against me and transmit notes and memoranda to the complainant had done their duty, they would have apprised him also that I had a habit of spanking the boys instead of lashing their backs with a cat or a colt [a rope whip], and he could have reported me for cruelty or unusual punishment on this count of the indictment.

I launched my bark on the stormy ocean of life as a cabin boy. I had no powerful interests to urge my promotion, no hereditary rank and power to build up claims, or friends at court to enroll my name on the list of favorites to be provided for. I did not jump from the drawing room, with ruffled shorts, perfumed locks and white kid gloves, into the wardroom, but in the constant labor and hardship of a seaman's life, studied, and I hope well and practically, a seaman's duty and a seaman's character.

Mr. President and gentlemen of the court, in all the charges against me on this trial, the affair of the boy Thompson is the only one to which the slightest importance can be attached, and I now proceed to shew that my conduct in that affair was entirely legal and comes within the purview of the regulations governing the navy. I read sir from the circular issued from the Navy Department, September 26, 1831:

Flogging is recommended to be discontinued when practicable by courts as well as officers, and some bade of disgrace, fine, etc., substituted where the discretion exists.

As this was a case of discretion, I exercised it humanely, as I conceived by a *badge of disgrace*, such as the instruction just read seems to indicate. The act therefore was legal, and also humane...

...Commencing, as I have before said, as a cabin boy, I made the character, temper and habits of seamen a close and particular study, and in the forecastle and yardarm had ample opportunities of ascertaining the peculiar characteristics of the sailor, and years of practical illustration had served to convince me that strict discipline, obedience to orders, sobriety, and a sense of duty can be secured without the constant, unwavering, and unflinching application of the lash for almost every offence. No one will deny, who are familiar with seamen, that an occasional use of the cat to the refractory cannot be dispensed with, but my own experience has led me to place a high estimate on the value of a mild and moral system, which sinks deep into the heart, without the necessity of lacerating the body, of using light punishments for subordinate offences, of efforts to create shame and regret by proper examples and salutary reproofs...

...It appeared in evidence on this trial that to punish a drunkard I did not put him in irons and allow him to beat his head and body on deck until he was bruised to a jelly and unfit for duty when he became sober, but placed him in a safe place, and when his senses were restored, I hung a wooden bottle around his neck on which "Drunkard" was inscribed. This may have been unusual, but it is not cruel, and the result satisfied me that shame will do more to correct intemperance than stripes. The incorrigible pilferer I punished by placing a wooden collar around his neck....

...Lieut. Downes testified before this court that he saw less punishment on board my ship than in any other, save one, that he had ever sailed in. I admit my aversion to the free and constant use of the cat, much less lacerating the backs of boys of tender age, covering them with stripes and blood and punishing them as hardened felons, and, therefore, governed by the discretion which the law allows the commander of a ship of war, I have studied and practiced all the reforms, which mildness could suggest, as substitutes for corporeal punishment, and it was under the same sense of duty that the light punishment inflicted on the boy Thompson was adopted, instead of the lash.

What, then, are the results of my system? No ship in the navy had a better or more orderly set of men, none obeyed orders more cheerfully, in no ship was there less severe punishment, and in none less manifestations of mutiny and disaffection. If I am to be censured for this course, for this departure from higher examples, I may regret it as unmerited, but it does not shake my faith in the system, nor my conviction that finally it will be the universal and successful one for the government of the navy.

Mordecai Manuel Noah:

(During America's war with the Barbary pirates, Noah's diplomatic mission to North Africa was to release certain New England fishermen by paying their ransom. A political furor arose surrounding his authority. He was charged with not notifying the State Department that his religion might interfere with his task.

President Madison, who assured him that his religion was not an impediment to his service to his government, later vindicated him. Noah wrote a book about his travels throughout Europe and North Africa. This excerpt explains his duties as the American consul to Tunisia.)

Letter from Secretary of State James Monroe April 25, 1815

Sir:

At the time of your appointment as consul at Tunis, it was not known that the religion which you profess would form any obstacle to the exercise of your consular functions. Recent information, however, on which entire reliance may be placed, proves that it would produce a very unfavourable effect. In consequence of which, the President has deemed it expedient to revoke your commission. On the receipt of this letter, therefore, you will consider yourself no longer in the public service. There are some circumstances, too, connected with your accounts, which require a more particular explanation, which, with that already given, are not approved by the President.

I am, very respectfully, sir,
Your obedient servant,
(signed) James Monroe.
Mordecai M. Noah, Esquire,
etc., etc.

From Noah's Memoirs:

[**The next day**] " ...I once more read the letter of Mr. Monroe. I paused to reflect on its contents. I was at a loss to account for its strange and unprecedented tenor: my religion an object of hostility? I thought I was a citizen of the United States, protected by the constitution in my religious, as well as my civil, rights. My religion was known to the government at the time of the appointment, and it constituted one of the prominent causes why I was sent to Barbary. If, then, any "unfavourable" events had been created by my religion, they should have been first ascertained, and not acting upon a supposition, upon imaginary consequences, have thus violated one of the most sacred and delicate rights of a citizen. Admitting, then, that my religion had produced an unfavourable effect, no *official* notice should have been taken of it. I could have been recalled without placing on file a letter thus hostile to the spirit and character of our institutions. ..

...What injury could my religion create? I lived like other consuls; the flag of the United States was displayed on Sundays and Christian holidays. The Catholic priest, who came into my house to sprinkle holy water and pray, was received with deference and freely allowed to perform his pious purpose. The barefooted Franciscan, who came to beg, received alms in the name of Jesus Christ. The Greek bishop, who sent to me a decorated branch of palm on Palm Sunday, received, in turn, a customary donation. The poor Christian slaves, when they wanted a favour came to me. The Jews alone asked nothing from me. Why then am I to be persecuted for my religion? Although no religious principles are known to the constitution, no peculiar worship connected with the government, yet I did not forget that I was representing a Christian nation. What was the opinion of Joel Barlow [U.S. Consul to Algiers, 1795], when writing a treaty for [Tripoli, 1797] one of the Barbary States? Let the following article, *confirmed by the Senate of the United States,* answer:

Article 11th – As the government of the United States of

America *is not, in any sense, founded on the Christian religion* – as it has, in itself, no character of enmity against the laws, religion, or tranquillity of Mussulmen [Mohammedans]; and as the said States never have entered into any war, or act of hostility against any Mahometan nation, it is declared by the parties, that no pretext arising from religious opinions shall ever produce an interruption of the harmony existing between the two countries.

If President Madison was unacquainted with this article in the treaty, which in effect is equally binding in all the States of Barbary, he should have remembered that the religion of a citizen is not a legitimate object of official notice from the government. And even admitting that my religion was an obstacle, and there is no doubt that it was not, are we prepared to yield up the admirable and just institutions of our country at the shrine of foreign bigotry and superstition? Are we prepared to disfranchise one of our citizens to gratify the intolerant view of the Bey of Tunis? Has it come to this, that the noble character of the most illustrious republic on earth, celebrated for its justice and the sacred character of its institutions, is to be sacrificed at the shrine of a Barbary pirate? Have we fallen so low? What would have been the consequence, had the Bey known and objected to my religion? He would have learnt from me, in language too plain to be misunderstood, that whoever the United States commissions as their representatives, he must receive and respect, if his conduct be proper. On that subject I could not have permitted a word to be said.

If such a principle is attempted to be established, it will lay the foundation for the most unhappy and most dangerous disputes. Foreign nations will dictate to us the religion which our officers at their courts should profess. With all the reflection, and the most painful anxiety, I could not account for this most extraordinary and novel procedure. Some base intrigue, probably one who was ambitious of holding this wretched office, had been at some pains to represent to the government that my religion would produce injurious effects, and the President, instead of closing the door on such interdicted subjects, had listened and concurred. And after having braved the perils of the ocean, residing in a barbarous country, without family or relatives, supporting the rights of the nation, and hazarding my life from poison or the stiletto, I find my own government, the only protector I can have, sacrificing my credit, violating my rights, and insulting my feelings, and the religious feelings of a whole nation. O! Shame, shame! The course which men of refined or delicate feelings should have pursued, had there been grounds for such a suspicion, was an obvious one. The President should have instructed the Secretary of State to have recalled me, and to have said that the causes should be made to me on my return. Such a letter as I received should never have been written, and, above all, should never have been put on file. But it is not true that my religion either had, or would have produced injurious effects. The Dey of Algiers had appointed Abraham Busnah his minister at the court of France; Nathan Bacri is Algerine consul at Marseilles; his brother holds the same office at Leghorn. The treasurer, interpreter, and commercial agent of the Grand Seigneur at Constantinople are Jews...

...It was not necessary for a citizen of the United States to have his faith stamped on his forehead. The name of freeman is sufficient passport, and my government should have supported me, had it been necessary to have defended my rights, and not to have themselves assailed them...after this, what nation may not oppress them?

That the subject of religion should ever have commanded the official notice of the government of the United States cannot fail to create the greatest surprise when a reference is had to the Constitution of the United States, and equally so to the enlightened state of the times. In the War for Independence the Jews were unanimous in their zealous co-operation, and we find them holding a high rank in the army and fighting for liberty with a gallantry worthy of the descendants of Joshua,

David and Maccabees. After the adoption of the constitution, we see them on the bench as judges, in the legislatures as members, and assisting the government, in gloomy periods, to regulate and strengthen the financial system...

...I will defend my rights and measures at every hazard, and will not permit the government to treat them lightly without a full and clear explanation. I have no reason to believe, neither would I wish to insinuate, that either the President or Secretary of State are desirous, by any official act, to disqualify a citizen, "give a sanction to bigotry," or awaken the most unhappy and unfortunate prejudices that can possibly exist, those of religion. It would be very inconsistent with their character, but the experiment is too dangerous to countenance ...

...The citizens of the United States who profess to the Hebrew religion have merited, by their exemplary conduct, the rights which they enjoy. They have been the constant, unwavering friends of the Union. They took an active part in the War of the Revolution, which secured, and ought to secure to them, an equality of privileges in common with the rest of their fellow-citizens. Forty years of freedom have strengthened and secured their attachment and devotion to a country which had broken down the barriers of superstition in proclaiming and perpetuating civil and religious liberty...

...If we once establish distinctions of religion in the appointment of our officers abroad, we shall not dare to send a Catholic to England, a Protestant to France, or a Jew to Spain, Instead of shameing by our liberality, and by the force of our noble institutions, these unworthy and destructive prejudices, we shall nourish them by the example unworthy [of] freemen and shall, in time, forget that distinction in religion, rank, rights, opinions, and privileges, are all absorbed in the honorable name of American.

Gratz family Petition to the United States Senate, Philadelphia, April 11, 1854:

(Rebecca Gratz would be considered an activist if she lived at the close of the 20th century. Her social conscience was honed by other members of her family, who also made public their positions on Civil Rights.

This excerpt is a petition to Congress signed by members and relatives of the Gratz family.)

To the Honorable the Senate of the United States.

The petition of the undersigned respectfully shows: that they are citizens of the United States professing the Jewish religion, and that their brethern in faith and fellow Citizens are often necessarily absent in Foreign lands. That when so absent, they are in very many instances deprived of most of their civil and religious rights, while the Citizens and subjects of the lands thus intolerant, enjoy under our laws, equal privileges with our Citizens.

Your petitioners therefore pray, that the attention of Government may be directed to this want of reciprocity in the rights accorded to Foreigners among us, and those extended to our Citizens in other Countries, and that in its wisdom it will endeavour to obtain for every American Citizen abroad, of every creed, a just degree of civil and religious freedom.

And your petitioners will ever pray, &c.

> Jo Gratz
> Isaac Hays
> Hor Etting
> Benj. Etting
> Jac. Gratz
> Hyman Gratz
> Philadelphia April 11th 1854

Judah Touro's Will

(Judah Touro's remarkable will, coming as it did when German Jewish migration was on the upswing, was welcome assistance to older communities which were coping with new members, and the newer communities which required help to organize themselves. In this excerpt, most of the organizations – Jewish and non-Jewish - that were the object of this benefactor's largesse appear. It is interesting to note that Touro gave money to every Jewish congregation but one, Cong. Beth Elohim of Charleston, the first Reform synagogue in the United States..

Imagine a similar benefactor dispensing money to all of the congregations and Jewish organizations today!)

New Orleans, January 6, 1854

Be it Known that on this Sixth day of January, in the year of our Lord One Thousand, Eight Hundred and Fifty Four, and of the Independence of the United States of America the Seventy Eighth at a quarter before Ten O'Clock A.M. ...

Personally appeared Mr. Judah Touro of this City, Merchant, whom, I the said Notary and said witnesses found setting in a room at his residence No. 128, Canal Street, Sick of body, but sound in mind, memory and Judgment as did appear to me, the said Notary and to said witnesses. And the said Judah Touro requested me, the notary, to receive his last will or Testament, which he dictated to me, Notary, as follows, to wit and in presence of said witnesses.

1st. I declare that I have no forced heirs.

2d. I desire that my mortal remains be buried in the Jewish Cemetery in New Port Rhode Island as soon as practicable after my decease.

3d. I nominate and appoint my trusty and Esteemed friends Rezin Davis Shepherd of Virginia, Aaron Keppel Josephs of New Orleans, Gershom Kursheedt of New Orleans, and Pierre Andre Destrac Cazenave of New Orleans, my Testamentary Executors and the detainers of my Estate, making, however, the following distinction between my said Executors, to wit: to the said Aaron Keppel Joseph, Gershom Kursheedt and Pierre Andre Destrac Cazenave, I give and bequeath to each one separately the sum of Ten Thousand dollars, which legacies, I intend respectively not only as tokens of remembrance of those esteemed friends, but also as in consideration of all Services they may have hitherto rendered me, and in lieu of the commissions to which they would be entitled hereafter in the capacity of Testamentary Executors as aforesaid. And as regards my other designated Executors, say my dear old and devoted friend the said Rezin Davis Shepherd to whom, under Divine Providence, I was greatly indebted for the preservation of my life, when I was wounded on the 1st of January 1815, I hereby appoint and institute him, the said Rezin Davis Shepherd, after the payment of my particular legacies and the debts of my succession, the Universal Legatee of the rest and residue of my estate, moveable and immoveable...

...6th. I give and bequeath to the Hebrew Congregation the ["]Dispersed of Judah" of the City of New Orleans, all that certain property situated in Bourbon Street immediately adjoining their Synagogue, being the present School house and the resident of the Said Mr. Gershom Kursheedt, the same purchased by me from the Bank of Louisiana; and also to the said Hebrew Congregation, the Two adjoining brick Houses purchased from the Heirs of David Urquhart, the revenue of said property to be applied to the founding and support of the Hebrew School connected, with Said congregation, as well to the defraying of the Salary of their Reader or Minister, Said Property to be conveyed accordingly by my said Executors to said congregation with all necessary restrictions.

7th. I give and bequeath to found the ["]Hebrew Hospital of

New Orleans" The entire property purchased for me, at the succession sale of the late C. Paulding upon which property the Building now Known as the "Touro Infirmary" is situated: The said contemplated Hospital to be organized according to law, as a charitable Institution for the relief of the Indigent Sick, by my Executors and such other persons as they may associate with them conformable with the laws of Louisiana.

8th I give and bequeath to the Hebrew Benevolent Association of New Orleans Five Thousand Dollars.

9th I give and bequeath to the Hebrew Congreation "Shangarar Chased" of New Orleans Five Thousand Dollars.

10th... to the Ladies Benevolent Society of New Orleans, the Sum of Five Thousand dollars.

11th... to the Hebrew Foreign Mission Society of New Orleans, Five Thousand Dollars.

12th...to the Orphans Home Asylum of New Orleans, the sum of Five Thousand Dollars.

13th... to the Society for the relief of Destitute Orphan Boys in the Fourth District, Five Thousand Dollars.

14th... to St Anna's Asylum for the relief of destitute females and children, the sum of Five Thousand Dollars.

15th... to the New Orleans Female Orphan Asylum at the corner of Camp & Prytania Streets, Five Thousand Dollars.

16th... to the St. Mary's Catholic Boys Asylum, of which my old & esteemed friend Mr. Anthony Rasch is chairman of its Executive Committee,...Five Thousand Dollars.

17th... to the Milnhe Asylum of New Orleans...Five Thousand Dollars.

18th... to the Fireman's charitable Association of New Orleans, Four Thousand Dollars.

19th... to the Seamen's Home in the First District of New Orleans, Four Thousand Dollars.

20th... for the purpose of establishing an Alms House, in the City of New Orleans, and with the view of contributing as far as possible to the prevention of mendicity in said city, the sum of Eighty Thousand Dollars (say $80,000.)...

21st I give and bequeath to the City of New Port in the State of Rhode Island, the Sum of Ten Thousand Dollars, on condition that the said sum be expended in the purchase and improvement of the property in Said City, Known as the "Old Stone Mill["] to be Kept as a public Park or Promenade ground.

22nd... to the Red Wood library of New Port aforesaid, for Books & Repairs Three Thousand Dollars

23... to the Hebrew Congregation Oharbay Shalome of Boston Massachusetts Five Thousand dollars.

24... the Hebrew Congregation of Hartford Connecticut Five Thousand dollars.

25... the Hebrew Congregation of New Haven Connecticut Five Thousand dollars.

26... the North American Relief Society for the Indigent Jews. Of Jerusalem Palestine of the City and State of New York (Sir Moses Montefiore of London, their agent) Ten Thousand Dollars, Say ($10,000.)

27. It being my earnest wish to cooperate with the said Sir Moses Montefiore of London, Great Britain, in endevouring to ameliorate the condition of our unfortunate Jewish brethern in the Holy Land, and to secure to them the inestimable privilege of worshipping the Almighty according to our Religion, without molestation, I therefore give and bequeath the sum of Fifty Thousand Dollars...

28. It is my wish and desire that the Institutions to which I have already alluded in making this Will, as well as those to which in the further course of making this Will, I shall refer, Shall not be disqualified from inheriting my legacies to them respectively made for reason of not being Incorporated ...

29... to the Jews Hospital Society of the City and State of New York Twenty Thousand Dollars.

30... to the Hebrew Benevolent Society Mashebat Nafesh of New York, Five Thousand dollars

31... to the Hebrew Benevolent Society Gimelet Chased of New York Five Thousand Dollars

32... to the Talmueh Torah School fund attached to the

Hebrew Congregation Sheareth Israel of the City of New York and to said Congregation Thirteen Thousand Dollars.

33... to the Educational Institute of the Hebrew Congregation Briai Jeshurum of the City of New York the sum of Three Thousand Dollars.

34... to the Hebrew Congregation Shangarai Tefila of New York Three Thousand Dollars.

35... to the Ladies Benevolent Society of the City of New York... Three Thousand Dollars.

36... to the Female Hebrew Benevolent of Philadelphia (Miss Gratz Secretary) Three Thousand Dollars.

37... to the Hebrew Education Society of Philadelphia (Pennsylvania) Twenty Thousand Dollars.

38... to the United Hebrew Benevolent Society of Philadelphia aforesaid Three Thousand Dollars.

39... to the Hebrew Congregation Ashabat Israel of Fells Point Baltimore, Three Thousand Dollars.

40... to the Hebrew Congreggation Beth Shalome of Richmond Virginia, Five Thousand dollars.

41... to the Hebrew Congregation Sheareth Israel of Charleston South Carolina the sum of Five Thousand Dollars.

42... to the Hebrew Congregation Shangarai Shamoyen of Mobile Alabama Two Thousand Dollars.

43... to the Hebrew Congregation Mikve Israel of Savannah Georgia Five Thousand Dollars.

44... to the Hebrew Congregation of Montgomery Alabama Two Thousand Dollars say ($2000).

45... to the Hebrew Congregation of Memphis Tennessee Two Thousand dollars.

46... to the Hebrew Congregation Adas Israel of Louisville Kentucky Three Thousand Dollars

47... to the Hebrew Congregation Braiai Israel of Cincinnati Ohio Three Thousand Dollars

48... to the Hebrew School Talmud Jeladin of Cincinnati Ohio Five Thousand Dollars.

49... to the Jewish Hospital of Cincinnati Ohio Five

Thousand Dollars.

50... to the Hebrew Congregation Tifareth Israel of Cleveland Ohio, Three Thousand Dollars.

51... to the Hebrew Congregation B'nai El of St Louis Missouri Three Thousand dollars.

52... to the Hebrew Congregation of Beth El of Buffalo New York Three Thousand dollars.

53... to the Hebrew Congregation of Beth El of Albany New York Three Thousand Dollars.

54... to the three following Institutions named in the Will of my greatly beloved brother the late Abraham Touro of Boston, the following sums.

First, To the Asylum for Orphan Boys in Boston Massachusetts, Five Thousand dollars.

Second, To the Female Orphan Asylum of Boston aforesaid Five Thousand Dollars.

Third, And to the Massachusetts General Hospital Ten Thousand Dollars.

55. I give and bequeath Ten Thousand dollars for the purpose of paying the salary of a Reader or Minister to officiate at the Jewish Synagogue of New Port Rhode Island and to endow the Ministry of the same as well as to keep in repair and embellish the Jewish Cemetery in New Port aforesaid; the said amount to be appropriated and paid or invested for that purpose in such manner, as my Executors may determine Concurrently with the Corporation of New Port aforesaid, if necessary; And it is my wish and desire that David Gould and Nathan H. Gould sons of my Esteemed friend the late Isaac Gould Esq of New Port aforesaid, should continue to oversee the Improvements in said Cemetery and direct the same, and as a testimony of my regard and in consideration of Services rendered by their Said Father, I give and bequeath the Sum of Two Thousand Dollars to be equally divided between them, the said David and said Nathan H. Gould. ...

...."Signed" J. Touro

Ernestine L. Rose: Speeches at the 3rd National Woman's Rights Convention, Syracuse, New York, September 8-10, 1852

Ernestine L. Rose, being introduced as a Polish lady, and educated in the Jewish faith, said –

It is of very little importance in what geographical position a person is born, but it is important whether his ideas are based upon facts that can stand the test of reason, and his acts are conducive to the happiness of society. Yet, being a foreigner, I hope you will have some charity on account of speaking in a foreign language. Yes, I am an example of the universality of our claims; for not American women only, but a daughter of poor, crushed Poland, and the downtrodden and persecuted people called the Jews, "a child of Israel," pleads for the equal rights of her sex. I perfectly agree with the resolution, that if woman is insensible to her wrongs, it proves the depth of her degradation. It is a melancholy fact, that woman has worn her chains so long that they have almost become necessary to her nature – like the poor inebriate, whose system is so diseased that he cannot do without the intoxicating draft, or those who are guilty of the pernicious and ungentlemanly practice of using tobacco until they cannot dispense with the injurious stimulant. Woman is in a torpid condition, whose nerves have become so paralyzed that she knows not she is sick, she feels no pain, and if this proves the depth of her degradation, it also proves the great wrong and violence done to her nature. ***

Woman is a slave, from the cradle to the grave. Father, guardian, husband – master still. One conveys her, like a piece of property, over to the other. She is said to have been created only for man's benefit, not for her own. This falsehood is the main cause of her inferior education and position. Man has arrogated to himself the right to her person, her property, and her children; and so vitiated is public opinion, that if a husband is rational and just enough to acknowledge the influence of his wife, he is called :hen-pecked." The term is not very elegant, but it is not of my coining; it is yours, and I suppose you know what it means; I don't. But it is high time these irrationalities are done away, for the whole race suffers by it. In claiming our rights, we claim the rights of humanity; it is not for the interest of woman only, but for the interest of all. The interest of the sexes cannot be separated – together they must enjoy or suffer – both are one in the race. ***

II
I wish to introduce a resolution, and leave it to the action of the Convention:

Resolved, That we ask not for our rights as a gift of charity, but as an act of justice. For it is in accordance with the principles of republicanism that, as woman has to pay taxes to maintain government, she has a right to participate in the formation and administration of it. That as she is amenable to the laws of her country, she is entitled to a voice in their enactment, and to all the protective advantages they can bestow; and as she is as liable as man to all the vicissitudes of life, she ought to enjoy the same social rights and privileges. And any difference, therefore, in political, civil and social rights, on account of sex, is in direct violation of the principles of justice and humanity, and as such ought to be held up to the contempt and derision of every lover of human freedom.

Photo Credits:

Map of New Amsterdam, c. 1642: Author's collection

Peter Stuyvesant: Museum of the City of New York

View of New Amsterdam, c. 1667: Author's collection

Exterior, Newport Synagogue, photo ©John T. Hopf

Interior, Newport Synagogue, photo © John T. Hopf

Dedication Plaque, Newport Synagogue, photo © John T. Hopf

Photograph of Washington's Letter, © John T. Hopf

Portrait of Abraham Touro by Gilbert Stuart, photo © by
John T. Hopf

Image of Savannah Georgia in 1778: Georgia Historical Society,
Savannah

Lorado Taft Sculpture of George Washington, Haym Salomon,
and Robert Morris: City of Chicago

Thomas Kennedy portrait: The Western Maryland Room,
Washington County Free Library, Hagerstown, Maryland

Cover, "Jew Bill": Jewish Museum of Maryland

Page from "Jew Bill": Jewish Museum of Maryland

Portrait, Uriah Phillips Levy: Dept. of the Navy, U.S. Naval
Academy Museum, Annapolis, Md.

Solomon Nunes Caravalho, self-portrait: Library of Congress,
LC-USZ62-61105

Indian Village, photo by Solomon Nunes Carvalho: Library of
Congress, LC-USZ62-9065

Portrait of "Abraham Lincoln and Diogenes" 1865, by Solomon
Nunes Carvalho: Rose Museum, Brandeis University

Waltham, Mass. Gift of Justin Turner, Los Angeles.

Ararat Stone: Buffalo & Erie County Historical Society,
   Buffalo, NY

Portrait of Rebecca Gratz as an older woman: American Jewish
   Historical Society, Waltham, Massachusetts and New York,
   New York

Thomas Scully portrait of the young Rebecca Gratz: Delaware
   Art Museum

Portrait of Judah Touro at Newport Synagogue, photo ©
   John T. Hopf

Portrait Isaac Lesser: National Museum of American Jewish
   History, Philadelphia

Portrait of Ernestine L. Rose: Schlesinger Library

Portrait Judah P. Benjamin: National Museum of American
   Jewish History, Phila.

BIBLIOGRAPHY

Baruch, Bernard M.: *Baruch: My Own Story*, Holt, New York 1957

Birmingham, Stephen: *The Grandees*. Harper & Row, New York, 1971

Bruce, Earl: *Synagogues, Temples and Congregations of Maryland 1830-1990*. Jewish Historical Society of Maryland, Baltimore, 1993

Cohen, Martin A., editor: *Sephardim in the Americas*. Hebrew Union College, American Jewish Archives, Cincinnati, 1996

De Sola Pool, David, editor and translator: *Book of Prayer According to the Custom of* the *Spanish and Portuguese Jews*, 2nd ed. 1979, New York

Encyclopedia Judaica, Jerusalem

Evans, Eli: *Judah P. Benjamin: The Jewish Confederate*. The Free Press, McMillian, New York, 1988

Ezratty, Harry A.: *500 Years in the Jewish Caribbean: The Spanish and Portuguese Jews in the West Indies*. Omni Arts, Inc., Baltimore, 1997

Faber, Eli: *A Time for Planting: The First Migration, 1654-1820*. Johns Hopkins University Press, Baltimore, 1992

Fein, Isaac M. *The Making of An American Jewish Community: The History of Baltimore Jewry from 1773 to 1920*. Jewish Historical Society of Maryland, 1971

Fitzpatrick, D. and Saphire, S.: N*avy Maverick: Uriah Phillips Levy.* Doubleday & Co., 1963.

Frazier, Nancy: *Jewish Museums of North America.* J. Wiley & Sons, New York, 1992

Friedman, Lee: *Jewish Pioneers and Patriots, 5th ed.* Jewish Publication Society of America, 1948

Friedman, Lee M.: *Pilgrims in a New Land.* Jewish Publication Society of America, Philadelphia, 1955

Gerber, Jane S.: *The Jews of Spain,* Free Press McMillan, 1992

Gilbert, Martin: *Jewish History Atlas.* McMillan & Co., London, 1969

Goldstein, Eric L.: *Traders and Transports, The Jews of Colonial Maryland,* Jewish Historical Society of Maryland, Baltimore, 1993

Grinstein, Hyman B.: *The Rise of the Jewish Community of New York 1654-1860.* Jewish Publication Society of America, 1945.

Hershkowitz, Leo: *Wills of Early New York Jews.* American Jewish Historical Society, New York, 1967

Korn, Bertram Wallace: *American Jewry and the Civil War.* Meridian Books, 1961

Korn, Bertram Wallace: *The Early Jews of New Orleans.* American Jewish Historical Society, 1969

Levitan, Tina: *The Firsts of American Jewish History.* Charuth Press, Brooklyn, New York, 1957

Libo K. and Howe, I.: *We Lived There Too.* St Martin's Press, Marek, New York 1984

Marcus, Jacob Rader: *American Jewry: Documents 18th Century.* Hebrew Union College Press, Cincinnati, 1959

Marcus, Jacob Rader: *Early American Jewry, 2 vols.* Jewish Publication Society of America, Philadelphia, 1951

Marcus, Jacob Rader: *Memoirs of American Jews, 1775-1865, 3 vols.* Jewish Publication Society of America, Philadelphia, 1955

Marks, M.L. : *Jews Among the Indians,* Benison Books, Chicago, 1992

Milgrim, Shirley: *Haym Solomon, Liberty's Son.* Jewish Publication Society of America, Philadelphia, 1971

Rochlin, Harriet and Fred: *Pioneer Jews*, Houghton Mifflin, 1984

Roth, Cecil: *A History of the Marranos.* Meridian Books/Jewish Publication Society of America, 1959

Sachar, Howard M.: *Farwell España: The World of the Sephardim Remembered.* Vintage Books, Random House, 1994

Sarna, Jonathan: *Jacksonian Jew: The Two Worlds of Mordecai Manuel Noah,* Holmes & Meier, 1981.

Schappes, Morris U.: *Documentary History of the Jews in the United States.* Citadel Press, N. Y. 1952 (revised edition)

Scharfman, Harold I.: *The First Rabbi,* Joseph Simon Pangloss Press, Malibu , California, 1988

Schoener, Allon: *The American Jewish Experience: From 1654 to the Present.* Museum of American Jewish History, Philadelphia, Pennsylvania, 1981

Sobel, Samuel, editor: *A Treasury of Jewish Sea Stories.* Jonathan David, New York, 1965

Sturhan, Joan: *Carvalho: Portrait of a Forgotten American.* Richwood Publishing Co., Merrick, N.Y. 1976

Touro Synagogue; Newport, R. I. The Society of Friends of Touro Synagogue, Newport, Rhode Island, 1948

Weintraub, Stanley: *Disraeli.* Truman Talley/Dutton, New York, 1993

Wiernek, Peter: *History of the Jews in America. 3rd edition.* Hermon Press, New York, 1972

Yaffe, James: *The American Jews.* Random House, New York, 1968

Young, Mel, editor: *Last Order of the Lost Cause.* University Press of America, Lanham, Maryland, 1995

Zara, Louis: *Blessed is the Land.* Crown, New York, 1954

Articles and Publications

Dalin, David G.: "Judaism's War on Poverty," Policy Review, Sept. and Oct., 1997

Lord, Lavis: "Matzos and Magnolias: The Lost World of Southern Judaism," U.S. News and World Report, May 25, 1996

Rezneck, Samuel: "The Strange Role of a Jewish Sea Captain in the Confederate South," American Jewish History, Vol. LXVIII, No. 1, 1978 (Jonas Levy, Uriah Levy's brother.)